Bermuda Real Estate

An In-Depth Guide to Bermuda Real Estate
and the Licensing Examination

First Edition
(with 2023 updates)

John R. Morgan

Morgan Testing Services
(www.MorganTestingServices.com)

ISBN-13   978-0-9791357-0-5
ISBN-10   0-9791357-0-2

Published by:

Morgan Testing Services
Post Office Box 231
Waterford, Connecticut 06385
www.MorganTestingServices.com
email: Bermuda@MorganTestingServices.com

We welcome reader comments about our text and test questions.
Please contact the publisher at the email address above regarding either.

Superintendent's Acknowledgments

The Superintendent of Real Estate would like to give special thanks in the production of this Bermuda-specific text to the author, Mr. John Morgan of Morgan Testing Services, Mrs. Karla Whitter of the Superintendent's office, and local realtors, Ms. Susan Thompson, Mrs. Ruby Dane, Ms. Jennifer Lindo, and Mr. Buddy Rego, who assisted with the reviews.

Author's Introduction

As a real estate student or instructor, some of the prelicensing textbook material you study makes you ask yourself that age-old question, "Will this be on the test?" As a general reader looking for some ready explanations of real estate principles and Bermuda real estate laws, you might simply wonder how applicable the material you are looking through is to Bermuda.

This book addresses those questions through a concentrated, no-nonsense approach to real estate principles and Bermuda laws that will provide you with answers to most of your basic questions. It has been crafted and reviewed with Bermudian readers in mind, and a special eye to preparing real estate professionals to have in-hand the basic knowledge expected of them.

To begin with, consider the natural flow of the Bermuda exam content outline: Its Section areas are logical and encompassing, and adaptable to content changes by using broad topic headings.

The outline begins where you are, with learning basic real estate terminology and concepts of property ownership, rights, and transfer (Section I). It then follows with terms, concepts, and processes common to Agency Relationships (Section II), which build on Section I.

Only after learning those basics can a person begin applying that knowledge to help a buyer or seller through the maze created by taking a real estate transaction from a desire to a deed transfer.

Sections III, IV, and V cover those principles, processes, and requirements that govern Bermuda licensees in their business practices while Section VI concentrates on the processes involved with real estate related portions of Acts, Amendments, and Policies found in Bermuda Laws.

As I have considered which terms and concepts are most logically associated with each Content Outline Topic Area, I have addressed them with the following principles in mind.
1. **Exam outline-area organization of key terms and concepts**
   - This means like-terms are clustered where they are most likely to be categorized for test use, regardless of where they may appear in a standard textbook presentation.
2. **Concise, direct definitions and descriptions**
   - This avoids over-explanation, especially where further elaboration could detract from the central, testable content. This book provides a focused review of both textbook and statutory materials. If you want more words, refer to a thick textbook or specific Bermuda law.
3. **Synonymous terms are presented together as "extra" terms**
   - This clarifies, as often as possible, that similar terms are, in fact, synonymous, and the way one textbook presented a topic may be tested with another term.
4. **Bold-faced and italicized identification of terms, definitions, and key phrases**
   - This serves to accentuate the more important content within a description or general statement. These formats will also highlight terms that may be used as *wrong answers*, known as "*distractors*" in the education and testing businesses, so unfamiliar terms will not trick you into thinking, "I should have studied that!"
5. **Related *nontestable* information is included, usually boldfaced and/or italicized**
   - This allows you to see more advanced, obscure, or regional information in the cluster of related material that, though inappropriate for testing, may appear as distractors.
6. **Italicized commentary**
   - This allows me to provide occasional conversational asides intended to further clarify a point, reduce potential topic-related anxiety, or stress nontestable topics.

Author's Introduction

7. **Minimal math emphasis**
   - This low emphasis is based primarily on the 5-10% emphasis of math on the exam, which makes math-related questions important, but not critical to one's overall score.

     This author is unapologetic about leaving math instruction to 500+ page textbooks. If you have weak math skills, you should work harder on them both now and under collegial supervision once you begin your career, but this book is not the drill and review text to strengthen them.

8. **Sufficient, not excessive, numbers of sample general questions**
   - The Sample Questions address central and critical topics adequately rather than exhaustively. The questions are patterned on the format used on the actual exam, and are typical of general questions drawn from principles and practices topics in Content Outline Areas I and II.
   - *NOTE:* Since the content presented in Content Outline Areas III-VI is based on the Licensing Act, Regulations, and Bermuda Laws which have been distilled to concise treatments of essential topics, *a close reading will suffice for exam preparation in these Areas* and *there will be no Sample Questions based on those topics.*

This book is designed with *brokers, licensees, the general public, prelicensing students, and instructors* in mind.

- **Brokers, licensees, and the general public** will find it useful as a light, handy, quick-reference book on terminology, concepts, and Bermuda laws applicable to the real estate practice and professional responsibilities.
- **Prelicensing students** will find it useful as a concise, comprehensive presentation of textbook principles and practices material in a test-outline format. And, since it distills the key terms and concepts presented in most standard texts, its usefulness will continue once you are licensed by serving as light, handy, quick-reference book!
- **Instructors** will find it a ready-made manual for a highly focused and effectively concentrated review of real estate principles and practices as well as Bermuda real-estate-related laws.

As a testing professional for over twenty years who is familiar with the Bermuda licence exam question bank, I am confident that the pool of questions, or "items," is sufficiently large and well-rounded to make the use of poorly written or "tricky" items both unnecessary and highly improbable. I am also confident that the questions used on exams provide a strong, representative sampling of the content domain of general real estate and Bermuda laws.

So, sorry: There are no shocking secrets to be revealed about "questions to watch out for." Everything herein is based on well-reasoned consideration of terms and concepts found during close reviews of over a dozen textbooks as well as numerous legal references, course curricula, and real estate job analysis reports.

My confidence in this book being the best one available rests primarily on my belief that the direct, concise presentation and organization of this text is grounded in unparalleled experience with real estate licensing examination subject matter and Subject Matter Experts internationally.

So, knowing what committees of Subject Matter Experts have concluded during dozens of review sessions does give me a refined sense of what would pass muster. And soon when *you* see a strange term and wonder, "Will this be on the test?" you, too, will know ***exactly*** what to say!

Publisher's Foreword and Note on Style

Since this Guide has been developed from close reviews of a wide selection of Real Estate Principles and Practices textbooks used in the United States to prepare candidates for the "general" portion of their respective jurisdiction's licensing examination, it will favor terms and practices common in the United States.

This will be most noticeable in Sections I and II, which are devoted to broadly applicable subjects that may differ in their finer details, such as local terminology, in different locales.

So, though most of the material discussed in Sections I and II is widely recognized as common fare within the extended real estate community, some of the terms and concepts may have no direct application or counterpart in Bermuda.

Wherever possible, the Bermudian reviewers have pointed this out and brought the presentation of extraneous material, such as American federal taxation and loan programs, to a minimum.

Also, periodically you will see Bermuda-specific shadow-text intended to clarify the Bermudian version of certain terms or processes, such as "compulsory purchase" for "eminent domain."

American-style spelling, punctuation, and general language usage will prevail, with a few exceptions, in the first two sections, but in the Bermuda-specific portion of the Exam Outline, Sections III-VI, every attempt has been made to observe conventions of usage and spelling common in Bermuda.

Perhaps the most obvious American/Bermudian "conflict" will be seen in the American spelling of "license" throughout Sections I and II which become transformed to "licence" with the mere turn-of-the-page from Section II to Section III.

> **Please take the time to contact the Superintendent or the Publisher with any comments regarding any of the material herein that might make this Guide more factually accurate, easier to understand, or appropriate for its Bermudian readers: We are anxious to incorporate such improvements in successive printings.**

Finally, the publisher wishes to make these important clarifications:

Nothing in this publication should be construed as indicating the Superintendent's responsibility for any of the author's interpretations, elaborations, or commentary on the Bermuda content outline's list of real estate topics.

All interpretations and elaborations of real estate subject matter are based on close research of standard texts, legal reference works, and government websites, along with textual revisions suggested by an international group of reviewers in the fields of real estate regulation, law, practice, and instruction.

All opinions regarding testing practices, policies, or procedures are those of the author based primarily on his professional test development training for preparing Scholastic Aptitude Test (SAT) Verbal sections and Advanced Placement (AP) Literature exams at the Educational Testing Service (ETS) and subsequent application of that training to real estate licensing programs in over twenty states and Bermuda. They are not necessarily shared currently by any other organization identified in this text.

Author's Dedication

This book is dedicated to the people of Bermuda for making a beautiful island a beautifully soul-nourishing place to live, even if simply during brief visits, as well as to the Ministry of Finance for offering this project to the people of Bermuda in sincere hopes Bermuda's future will be enhanced by making those who practice real estate better prepared to do so.

This edition is further dedicated to my brother, the solo circumnavigator Brechin "Brec" Morgan, whose voyage brought me to Bermuda in November 1998 to meet him as he finished a harrowing first leg from New England aboard Otter, his 27' Pacific Seacraft Orion.

Brec left from St. George on a trip that took him safely around the world and back to Bermuda in May 2003 through far-flung places that befit the Bermuda motto, "Whither the Fates carry us."

On his return layover in Bermuda he solicited insights from various Bermudians to assist his reentry to land-life, and one told him, "Think of the fish. It swims in salt water all its life, yet when you cook it, you have to add salt. Be in your environment and do not take it inside."

Brec's family and friends were all relieved that he and Otter made it back to Block Island (known on t-shirts there as "The Bermuda of the North") May 17, 2003 safely and in good health.

To date he has been mindful of the Bermudian's advice and has not salted his insides.

Content Outline for the Bermuda Real Estate Licensing Exam
100 questions for both Agent and Broker exams
This exam will include 5-10 questions on real estate mathematics and computations

Topics	# of questions

I. Principles and Practices of Real Estate (40 questions)
  A. Interests in Real Property
  B. Planning and Zoning
  C. Property Valuation
  D. Contracts (e.g., basic contract law, listings, sales, leases, options)
  E. Financing, Types of Loans, and Loan Provisions
  F. Mortgages, Deeds, and Title Issues
  G. Settlement/Closing
  H. Property Management and Investments

II. Law of Agency (15 questions)
  A. Definitions and Types of Agency
  B. Fiduciary Duties
  C. Characteristics of Agency Relationships
  D. Creation and Termination of Agency

III. Powers and Duties of the Superintendent of Real Estate (5 questions)
  A. Powers of the Minister
  B. Duties of the Superintendent
  C. Examination of Records/Audit
  D. Investigations, Notices, and Appeals
  E. Offences and Penalties

IV. Licensing Requirements (5 questions)
  A. Activities Requiring a Licence
  B. Exemptions
  C. Eligibility for Licensing
  D. Licence Renewal
  E. Notice of Change in Licence

Topics	# of questions

V. Statutory Requirements Governing the Activities of Licensees (15 questions)
  A. Advertising
  B. Broker/Agent Relations
  C. Remuneration
  D. Disclosure
  E. Handling of Documents
  F. Handling of Monies
  G. Listings
  H. Record Keeping
  I. Unfair Inducement
  J. Display of Licence

VI. General Aspects of Bermuda Property Law (20 questions)
  A. The Development and Planning Act 1974
    1. Part VI - Subdivisions
  B. The Conveyancing Act 1983
  C. The Land Valuation and Tax Act 1967
    1. Annual Rental Values - ARV
  D. The Stamp Duties Act 1976
    1. Conveyance and Transfer
    2. Appraisement
    3. Leases
    4. Mortgages
  E. The Rent Increases (Domestic Premises) Control Act 1978
  F. The Bermuda Immigration and Protection Act 1956
    1. Policy regarding the acquisition of Real Property by non-Bermudians
  G. The Landlord and Tenant Act 1974
  H. The Human Rights Act 1981

More extensive treatments of general real estate principles identified and tested in Sections I and II can be found in most basic, introductory real estate texts.

The source of Bermuda laws for Sections III-VI can be found on-line at www.BermudaLaws.bm; this is an excellent and very accessible site for confirming you have the most up-to-date information.

Table of Contents

[The rest of this page is intentionally left blank]

NOTE: The material presented throughout this Content Outline Area is based largely on real estate principles textbooks and legal dictionaries published in the United States. However, most terms, definitions, and concepts have been confirmed as applicable in Bermuda through both editorial input from Bermuda professionals and reference to the Oxford University Press's <u>A Dictionary of Law</u>.

In cases where they differ based on Bermuda legislative distinctions, the Bermuda-specific particulars are covered and tested in Content Outline Area VI, General Aspects of Bermuda Law. Also, in this Area, some Bermuda-specific terms and laws will be entered where appropriate in boxes like this one.

<u>Any test question from this Area that differs from the information below under Bermuda law, as presented in Area VI, will observe Bermuda law.</u>

However, those terms and concepts that do NOT apply in Bermuda will not be used as the "key," or correct answer, on the Bermuda licensing exam and are included below for informational purposes about the real estate profession.

I-A. Interests in Real Property

Definitions, descriptions, and ways to hold title

1. Elements of real and personal property

Real property, or *realty*, is *land along with its improvements*, things attached to it, and the benefits, rights, and interests included in its ownership.

> *Real property* and *real estate* are widely acknowledged as synonymous terms. However, *"real property"* is generally the preferred usage whenever it helps distinguish specific types of property as *real* instead of *personal* by avoiding the word *"estate,"* which, in its broadest sense, means everything one owns, including both real and personal property.

> *Land* includes the *earth's surface, subsurface to the center of the earth, the space overhead, and the rights to each*.

Three commonly recognized *physical characteristics of land* are its *immobility*, *permanence* (or *indestructibility*), and *uniqueness*.

> *All three of these characteristics can be illustrated by the simple example of a global positioning satellite (GPS) reading at a particular spot: the latitude and longitude reading for that spot cannot be moved, destroyed, or duplicated.*

Improvements are generally seen as additions to the property that increase its value or enhance its appearance and may include attached property, such as a house, garage, or fixtures, such as a sink or built-in bookcases, as well as trees, gardens, and landscaping.

*The opposite of improvements is **waste**, which is the legal term for property deterioration, abuse, or destruction, generally by a negligent tenant.*

Personal property, also known as *personalty* or *chattel*, is generally considered anything that is **unattached and moveable**, such as furniture, housewares, and throw rugs.
- *Personal property also includes various **intangible assets**, like **bank accounts**, **stocks**, and many other **securities and financial instruments**.*

Fixtures are once-moveable items that have been attached to real property. Since attaching the object *may* change its status from personal to real property, as with a sink, a ceiling fan, or even a coat hook screwed to the back of a door, tenants and those selling their property must be careful about how they install items they may want to take away with them.

Trade fixtures are fixtures used by a business tenant, such as display cases or supermarket freezers, that are generally considered the tenant's removable personal property.

Annexation is the term for how, by attachment, something that was formerly personal property becomes real property. Also referred to as *accession*, which includes additions to real property from natural causes, such as a riverfront property that benefits from a shift in the river's path, or artificial causes, such as new buildings or plantings on a property.

Severance refers to the process of separating a fixture from the real property, thereby changing it *from real to personal* property.

The legal tests for a fixture include considering the total circumstances of these four elements to determine whether or not the fixture is real or removable property
1. *intention* of the person who attached the item to make it permanent
2. *method of attachment*, or *annexation*, generally meaning the degree of permanence
3. *adaptation* of the item to the use of the property, as in a custom-made bookshelf that fits precisely into a recessed area and is attached with bolts
4. *relationship and general understanding* between parties, as in whether the owner paid for and installed the fixture, or a tenant has done so at the tenant's expense with the owner's permission to remove it later

Appurtenances are those things that "belong" to something else, generally by *attachment*, and in real estate generally include any number of rights that "*run with the land*," which means the rights do not end when a new owner takes title. Common examples include certain *easements*, such as deeded rights-of-way, and water rights.

Emblements are cultivated crops that a tenant generally owns as personal property and may return to harvest even after a lease expires.

*Growing crops are technically referred to as **fructus industriales** ("fruits of industry"), which distinguishes them from other plants, **fructus naturales** ("fruits of nature"), such as trees and brush, which are generally considered real property.*

*These terms are popular **distractors** – the testing industry's term for "wrong answers" that will distract the less-prepared – and are way too advanced for entry-level tests. You are more likely to have a personal encounter with a living American president than with these terms during the course of a lengthy real estate career.*

Additional "distractor" terms related to classes and characteristics of property include
- *tangible (or corporeal) property, which means **physically touchable, material** characteristics, most notably **land and its improvements,** and*
- *intangible (or incorporeal) property, which means such abstract, "untouchable," yet very real elements as **mortgages, rights, and other encumbrances, as well as assets such as bank accounts and most financial instruments, like stocks and retirement accounts.***

Do NOT expect to be tested on definitions or examples of tangible, intangible, corporeal, and incorporeal property, since these terms, though they provide useful distinctions, are more legally refined than is appropriate for an entry-level exam.

2. Property description and legal description

Although there are currently no enforced standards for *property descriptions* or *legal descriptions* in Bermuda, there are some basic commonly observed conventions for *boundary surveys* that are based on *metes and bounds* descriptions of separate properties as well as a *lot and block* method of identifying *parcels in a subdivision*.

Metes and bounds descriptions have been widely used in England for centuries, and are commonly used still wherever English common law held sway. Put simply, it describes a distinct property's boundary by identifying a *point of beginning (POB)* and then describing the distances *("metes")* and directions along the property line *("bounds")*, generally, but not always, following a clockwise direction around the entire property back to the POB.

A *monument* is any of a number of landmarks that provides a stable point of reference for surveys. They can be natural, such as "the south face of the stone outcropping at the base of the hill," or artificial, such as stone boundary markers (a.k.a. *merestones*) or surveyors' stakes, or bolts, generally marked with red witness pegs.

Lot and block descriptions are commonly used to describe particular parcels in a subdivision, so combine a metes and bounds description of distances between specific monuments, or reference points, and unique parcel identifier within the subdivision, such as *Lot 9*. A *subdivision map* will not only show the dimensions and boundary lines of each lot, but also identify access roads, easements, and other rights of way (ROWs).

*In Bermuda, professional **Boundary Surveys** typically mark private boundaries in red, ROWs in yellow, and other overlaps or entitlements in green.*

*Also, since **Bermuda property conveyances were not required to be registered until the Land Title Registration Act 2011 commenced in 2018**, every property owner maintained a collection of **Title Deeds** that shows the chain of ownership up to the current owner. Now that the **Land Title Registration Act 2011** is in effect, registration of these deeds will make maintaining the packet of originals legally redundant. Until a particular property has been registered, **originals are crucial** and must show that an individual has **at least twenty years' worth of deeds and/or transfer records** in order to legally convey a property; lost or damaged deeds can make a property both unmarketable and unmortgageable.*

3. Estates in real property

As noted above, in its broadest sense, *estate* simply means everything one owns, ***including both real and personal property***.

> ***Estates in real property,*** or ***estates in land,*** can be either ***freehold***, which means owned property, or ***nonfreehold***, also known as ***leasehold***, which means leased property.
>
> ***Leaseholds***, *including why they are classified as **personal property**, will be covered in Sections I-D and I-H, which elaborate on leasehold estates, leases, and property management topics.*

Title refers to both the ***ownership*** of something as well as to the ***legal evidence of ownership***, such as a ***deed***.

The degree and type of ownership gives rise to a variety of ***types of title***, though the primary one most often mentioned in the marketing and transfer of ownership is
- ***absolute title,*** or ***clear title***, or ***good title***, which refers to a title ***free of restrictions that would limit its transfer***

*The **bundle of rights**, or **bundle of legal rights**, is a common illustration of property ownership that compares the entire set of ownership rights to a bundle of sticks. (The bundle contains private rights; the government reserves additional rights to itself.)*

> *Each stick represents a separate, distinct ownership right, such as the right to possess and use it, exclude others from it, and rent, sell, or mortgage it.*
>
> *As any stick is given over to someone else, the absolute and complete ownership is increasingly limited by those who now control a "stick."*

Freehold estates commonly imply *fee simple*, or *absolute and complete ownership of real property*. The key distinctions for testing are that a freehold estate may or may not include conditions on its use and/or transfer.

If there are *no conditions on its use and/or transfer*, it may be known by any of these interchangeable terms: *fee*, *fee simple*, *fee simple absolute*, or *estate in fee simple*.

Note: This is the first of many cases to come in this book in which <u>Black's Law Dictionary</u> (10th ed. 2014) confirms that different terms are synonymous. (Please refer back to the Introduction for the purpose of providing "extra" terms where applicable throughout this book.)

A *life estate* is another category of estates in property, one that conveys an estate for the duration of the life of the *life tenant*. For example, a parent may deed the family home to an heir but retain the right to use the property for life. Or a husband may will his wife a life estate in a house they share for the duration of her life with it going to his children from a previous marriage upon her death.

There are a few related terms for life estates, including
- *future interests*, which refers to the right to acquire the estate upon its termination as a life estate. This typically takes one of the following two forms
  - *reversion*, or *reversionary interest*, which means the estate reverts to, or is returned to, the grantor of the life estate, who is known as a *reversioner*
  - *remainder*, or *remainder interest*, which means the grantor of the life estate has named someone else to take title; such an individual is referred to as a *remainderman*

*Offering opinions or interpretations, or preparing documents, on these matters could subject you to a suit for **practicing law without a license**. **Always tell clients to get a legal opinion on legal details from a practicing attorney.***

4. Voluntary and involuntary transfer/alienation of title to real property

The *transfer*, or *alienation*, or *conveyance* of title to property ownership from one party or entity to another can be categorized as being either *voluntary* or *involuntary*.

*The terms **transfer** and **alienation** are interchangeable, so either one may appear in test questions; **alienation** is used almost exclusively when property transfers are **involuntary**.*

Voluntary transfer refers to the free-will transfer of property by its owner using methods such as
- *deeding* it after selling it or making it a gift
- *assigning* it to another
- *dedicating* it for public use
- *willing* it to an heir

It is worth noting here that ***real property ownership is transferred by a deed***, while the ***transfer of personal property*** is formally accomplished through a ***bill of sale***. Both provide ***evidence*** that ***title*** has also been passed.

Property ***dedication*** refers to the donation of private property for public use. For example, a developer may ***dedicate*** roads and some common-use areas in a subdivision as part of its plan, so the municipality will own and maintain them.

Also, if the public uses ***nondedicated*** private land as if it were public, the property may become subject to an easement, much like a prescriptive easement, and legally turn into ***dedicated property***.

Note: In Bermuda, there are privately owned roads, public places, and sections of sidewalks that the owners will close off to the public one day a year to demonstrate that public use has been allowed under a revocable license. By doing this, the owner helps avoid loss of control through a claim of dedication.

The ***transfer of property by inheritance*** involves some terms that are worth noting here. Some of these are
- ***testate*** refers to having a will; a ***testator*** is someone who has made a will
- ***intestate*** refers to a situation where a person dies without a valid will
- ***probate*** is the public, legal process of executing the terms outlined in a will, or determining how to settle the estate if there is no will
  - ***personal representative*** is increasingly used for the person designated to see that the terms of a will are carried out; or the following names may apply
    - an ***executor*** is/was the term for a personal representative ***appointed by the testator in the will*** to execute the terms of the will; the term ***executrix*** refers to a female representative, *though **executor** is increasingly used in a gender-neutral way to identify this position*
    - an ***administrator*** is/was the term for a personal representative ***appointed by probate when someone died intestate, or when there is a will and the court sees a reason to appoint an administrator***; the term ***administratrix*** refers to a female representative, *though **administrator** is increasingly used in a gender-neutral way to identify this position*
  - ***intestate succession*** refers to the distribution of an estate that is not governed by a will, and follows applicable ***laws of descent and distribution*** (or ***devise and descent***) for ***intestacy***
    - ***escheat***, as noted above, is the process of property reverting to the government in the event someone dies intestate and with no heirs
- ***types of wills*** include
  - ***formal***, *or witnessed, which are typically prepared with the help of an attorney*
    - ***Though this is by far the most common will known in Bermuda,*** *there are also* ***oral***, *or* ***nuncupative***, *wills which are spoken by the person who is near death*

> *and written down by a witness, and **holographic**, or handwritten and unwitnessed wills. These wills are largely unknown in Bermuda, but possible as attempts to make one's final wishes known.*

- <u>**real**</u> **property disposed of in a will** is known as a **devise**; the recipient is a **devisee**
- <u>**personal**</u> **property disposed of in a will** is known as a **legacy** or **bequest**; the recipient is a **legatee**
- **real property transfers** to a devisee, or a buyer in order to settle estate obligations, may be **conveyed by** an **executor's deed** or an **administrator's deed**, depending on whether or not there is a will; *jurisdiction-specific terms for the instrument that transfers title of a deceased owner vary, and include such alternate terms as **certificate of devise, descent, or distribution** -- check with a real estate attorney for the term(s) that apply to any circumstance you may personally encounter*

Involuntary transfer, or **involuntary alienation**, refers to any situation where **title transfers** in a manner that the owner may not have any control over or would generally prefer not to have happen. Examples of these would include

- **foreclosure** due to financial default, including tax sales
- **condemnation** through the process of **eminent domain**
   > ***In Bermuda, eminent domain, or the taking of property by the government for a public purpose, is known as "compulsory purchase"**; see the **Acquisition of Land Act 1970** for more (www.BermudaLaws.bm).*
- **escheat** due to an owner's dying intestate with no heirs
- **adverse possession** as a result of **open, notorious, and hostile** use of a property for a statutory period; *this is generally **20 years** in Bermuda, but is extinguished if not exercised within 10 years of becoming eligible—consult a lawyer for specific requirements*
- **partition** by a court-ordered sale of a property with multiple owners, one or more of which cannot get the other(s) to buy their interest, and so petition the court to force a sale in order to receive their share of the proceeds
- **reversion** due to a breach in the terms of the deed or contract

Foreclosure is an area of special note since it is the most common recourse for lenders, and refers to the legal proceeding initiated by certain property creditors to **force the sale of a property in default of a loan or arrears in taxes in order to repay the debt**.

A foreclosure sale is an example of **involuntary alienation**, or **involuntary transfer**, **of property ownership**.

Foreclosure types and processes are too varied and jurisdiction-specific to address here, though it is worth noting that the two-party mortgage and the three-party deed of trust have different basic sets of processes. *Generally, the processes are known, respectively, as **judicial**, which means by a legal action in court that results in **a sale by court order**, or **writ of execution**, and **nonjudicial**, which means things proceed **according to contract terms alone**.*

*At a settlement for a foreclosure sale, the **priority of liens**, or the order of repayment to creditors with the sale proceeds, is important; if the proceeds do not cover all property liens, the creditors may be entitled to seek a **deficiency judgment** against the foreclosed property owner.*

Depending on the particular circumstances under which a foreclosure or other involuntary alienation occurs, some form of the following types of **protections** and/or **remedies** for **the owner** may come into play.

Since many of the following terms, concepts, and processes are not uniformly available or applied, they are provided for informational purposes and may be used on exams as distractors.

Some common terms associated with involuntary alienation protections and remedies include
- **redemption**, *which refers to the right to pay off a debt, even after mortgage default, and reclaim the property*
  - **redemption rights** *generally vary, but may include a before-foreclosure-sale right known as the **equitable right of redemption**, or even a statutory period after a sale, known as a **statutory right of redemption***
- a *deed in lieu of foreclosure*, or *deed in lieu*, refers to a situation in which the owner gives a lender the deed rather than going through a foreclosure proceeding; this is commonly known as a *"friendly foreclosure"*
- *forbearance* refers to a remedy by which the creditor refrains from taking legal action against a borrower in default after being satisfied that the borrower is taking acceptable measures to satisfy the debt. This is commonly referred to as *workout*.

5. Forms, rights, interests, and obligations of ownership

A quick introduction to the "Who's Who" in the legalese of real estate.

Entities, or *parties*, involved in a real estate transaction may be businesses as well as individuals. They take on special names depending on their relationship in a transaction.

The *–er (-or)*/*-ee* distinction, as in employer/employee, is applied to a host of pairings in real estate transactions. Matched pairs will appear where they best apply throughout this book. For here, though, the following are worth noting
- a *vendor* is the party that offers something for sale or trade, or actually sells something; a *vendee* is the purchaser
- an *offeror* is the party that offers something, an *offeree* is the one to whom it is offered
- a *charger,* or *mortgagor,* is *the owner* of property that is being put up as collateral for a loan; the *chargee,* or *mortgagee,* is *the lender*, personal or institutional, that finances the loan

Since the terms above, and others using the -er/-ee formations, do appear on various transaction-related documents in the normal course of business, *some of them may show up on a test as simple definition questions*.

Most unfamiliar terms that identify parties to a transaction should be pretty easy to figure out on sight if you look at the main word and think through what the –er(-or)/-ee endings mean.

Forms of ownership: Ways to "take title," or "hold title"

Sole ownership, or ***tenancy in severalty***, or simply ***severalty***, means that an individual is the sole owner of a property.

Concurrent ownership, or ***co-ownership***, refers to ownership by two or more parties at the same time. Among the types of concurrent ownership are

- ***tenancy in common***, under which the parties, or ***tenants in common***, hold an ***undivided fractional interest in the property***. For example, three family members may own a house together as equal one-third owners, or two may own 25% each and the third owns the remaining 50%. In either case, the fractional interest does not convey either the use or ownership of separate thirds, quarters, or halves of the house itself or its physical land to any of them. Also, ***each tenant may hold a deed that does not name any of the other owners***; *compare with* ***unity of title*** *below*.

- ***joint tenancy***, under which the parties, or ***joint tenants***, hold an ***undivided equal interest*** rather than uneven shares. The following considerations apply to this form of ownership
  - the ***four unities***, which refers to the following set of legal requirements for creating a joint tenancy
    - ***unity of interest***, which means all parties have an ***equal interest***
    - ***unity of possession***, which means all parties have ***undivided possession and use rights***
    - ***unity of time***, which means all parties ***took title at the same time***
    - ***unity of title***, which means all parties are ***named on the same deed***
  - the ***right of survivorship***, meaning that as each individual joint tenant passes away, the remaining tenants' interest would increase until ***the last remaining person becomes the sole owner***; this condition is ***historically an assumed part*** of a joint tenancy, and ***some older deeds will specify "as joint tenants and not as tenants in common"***
    - *this form of ownership is occasionally referred to as* ***"a poor man's will,"*** *and is often chosen by married couples to ensure that a surviving spouse automatically acquires full title upon the death of the other spouse*
    - *a joint tenancy's four unities, and the subsequent right of survivorship, can be turned into a tenancy in common through* ***severance***, *a process by one or more of the co-owners to alter the terms, thus allowing individual control over their respective proportionate interest*

Common interest ownership is a type of ownership that generally refers to multiple owners having an overlapping, inseparable interest in a property complex; ***condominiums and timeshares*** are the most common examples and will be discussed below

Forms of ownership: Some common interest and corporate ownership structures

Condominium ownership grants the owner (1) **fee simple title to the unit** <u>and</u> (2) **an undivided interest in the jointly owned common areas as tenants in common** with the other association members.

The **condominium** form of community ownership also has several components that often go by a variety of similar names.

Condominium status is achieved when a developer's organizational plans, widely known as the **declaration**, are recorded. The declaration typically includes a copy of the **bylaws** *(or bye-laws in Bermuda)*, **legal descriptions and surveys**, which identifies common areas as well as units, and a list of **restrictive covenants**, also known as the **covenants, conditions, and restrictions.**

In addition, the developer typically creates a **condominium owner's association** for the self-governing of the property by the unit owners. This association is responsible for ongoing upkeep and maintenance of common areas, which it funds by assessing and collecting each unit's proportionate share of cost through **association fees**, or **maintenance fees**

The local tax authority taxes the unit owner directly for the assessed value of the unit. Like an owner of a detached residence, **the unit owner is directly and solely responsible for taxes**: the association has no liability for unpaid unit taxes.

> *In Bermuda, the particulars of condominium creation and ownership are presented in the **Condominium Act 1986**, **Condominium General Regulations 1987**, and the **Condominium Amendment Act 1998**; refer to these laws for Bermuda-specific application of the above general description.*

Timeshare ownership is typically characterized by **fee simple ownership** of **interval occupancy of a specified unit**, although it may take the legal form of a right-to-use contract that simply conveys **a contractual fixed-year, recurring-use** of a specific unit.

Either way, the unit, generally an apartment unit at a resort property, is available to the owner for the specified period every year, such as the first week of June. It may also involve being able to "bank" the week and exchange it for a week at a different participating timeshare site.

> *In Bermuda, a timeshare property is referred to as a "timesharing scheme" and particulars are presented in the **Timesharing (Licensing and Control) Act 1981** and related subsequent regulations and amendments; refer to these laws for Bermuda-specific application of the above general description.*

Corporate and business ownership structures are generally more intricate than those sketched above. For office buildings, professional complexes, and other commercial ventures, there are a variety of **partnerships**, such as a **syndicate**, **joint venture**, or a **limited liability corporation (or company) (LLC)**, among others, that are simply *more complicated than entry level licensees are likely to encounter or be expected to know in detail.*

I. Principles and Practices of Real Estate   (40 questions)

Basic physical rights in land

At the outset of this section, *land* was described as including the surface, subsurface to the center of the earth, the space overhead, and the rights to each. Some broad categories identifying the most common rights in land include *surface rights*, *subsurface rights, mineral rights*, *water rights*, and *air rights*.

An owner is entitled to handle each of these rights separately and may, for example, lease out the right to farm the land as well as erect a billboard, respectively, to two separate parties.

Bermuda, being a group of coral islands, differs from most countries in its basic availability of the rights noted above.

Regarding *water rights*, *Bermuda still observes the Crown Right* known as *"the Queen's Bottom,"* which refers to *government ownership of the seabed* stretching from the *mean high water mark*, or line, *outward for twelve nautical miles*.

This means that waterfront property owners have no entitlement to construct docks or piers; rather, they must adhere to all applicable government regulations.

Key terms related to administering coastal rights and the Queen's Bottom include
- *foreshore refers to the intertidal zone, from the lowest to the highest level reached by waves; sometimes referred to at the **Queen's Foreshore**, and includes a lot of beaches*
- *foreshore encroachments refer to docks or other structures that extend over and/or beyond the foreshore, generally ending over the seabed in navigable water*
- *foreshore leases refer to leases and licenses for the foreshore and seabed issued by the Ministry of Public Works' Department of Public Lands and Buildings, **generally for 21 years***

I-B. Planning and Zoning

Public Controls on Planning and Zoning (e.g., zoning, taxation, police power)

Public controls and restrictions on property are embodied primarily in what are commonly referred to as *the four government* (or *governmental*) *powers*. *Many of these powers, such as the imposition of tax liens or the process of escheat, take effect by **operation of law**, which means automatically, without any action, knowledge, or approval required of the owner.*

The *four government powers* are *police power*, *taxation*, *eminent domain*, and *escheat*.

*As noted above, eminent domain is **known in Bermuda** as **"compulsory purchase"** and detailed in the **Acquisition of Land Act 1970**.*

Police power refers to the government's authority to provide for the general welfare of the community through legislation and a range of *enabling acts*, or *enabling statutes*, that authorize agencies to organize and both implement and enforce their obligations.

Zoning is a type of police power under which municipalities can regulate land use. This begins with a *master plan*, or *comprehensive plan*, or *general plan*, which identifies the broad economic objectives and goals and seeks to achieve them through classifying certain areas or buildings as usable for specific purposes, such as residential, retail, industrial, and agricultural.

Nonconforming use in zoning refers to a property *continuing a prior use after a zoning change*. For example, a commercial area that has been rezoned residential may include a building that has a corner grocery. It may continue to sell groceries, though if it closes, it may have to be converted into residential space.

A common residential example would be *an existing house on a small lot in a neighborhood that has been rezoned* to require at least one acre for new construction. The house will generally be *"grandfathered"* and allowed to remain on its now "substandard" lot; typically it can be rebuilt if destroyed.

A *variance* also allows for a use other than the primary zoning category, but is *granted after review by the zoning authorities*. Examples include opening a restaurant in a residential area or a hairdressing salon in a renovated portion of a family residence.

A *conditional use*, or *special use*, is similar to a variance, but differs primarily in that it is typically more restrictive, and therefore governed by a *permit* that can be revoked if the holder does anything not specifically allowed.

Spot zoning is also similar to a variance, but differs in that the parcel or small *area in question is actually rezoned* to allow it to coexist within an area of different zoning requirements.

Other common zoning terms include
- *setback*, or the specified distance a building must be from a property line
- *buffer zone*, or area that serves to separate one use from another, as when an open stretch is required to separate a new industrial park and an existing school
- *zoning orders*, which are simply municipal regulations governing zoning and land-use requirements
- *building codes*, which are governed by zoning orders and outline the local requirements for construction standards

Environmental regulations are public controls grounded in the government's *exercise of police power*.

Taxation is a government power necessary to raise revenue for municipal expenses, like schools and roads; the governmental right to set taxes allows a municipality to assess properties, levy taxes, and sell individual properties when their taxes go unpaid.

I. Principles and Practices of Real Estate   (40 questions)

Typically, real property is assigned an **assessed value** by the municipal government's assessor's office that is then used as the basis for annual taxation for **general assessments**, which raise funds for the entire municipality.

> **In Bermuda,** *this is known as **annual rental value (ARV)**; see VI-C for more.*

These **general real estate taxes** are also called **ad valorem** taxes, which means they are taxed **"at value,"** so that properties with a higher assessed value pay proportionately more than those with a lesser value.

A property may also be subject to **special assessment** taxes if there are certain improvements, such as neighborhood sidewalk construction or streetlight installation, that benefit the immediate area only.

> *Practical note: assessed values for tax purposes rarely match, or even intend to match, a property's actual, current, fair market value, although the two are commonly confused by the general public. One reason for this is that the assessment values may remain unchanged for years, whereas current market values are subject to constant change.*

The governmental **power of taxation includes the power to place liens** on property in the event of an outstanding special assessment or unpaid general taxes.

Eminent domain *(known in Bermuda as **compulsory purchase**)* is another government power. It refers to the **taking** of title to real property for some use, public or private, that has been judged by the appropriately authorised governmental entity to be beneficial to the community's interest, as with certain utility or industrial expansions, or civic improvements.

Eminent domain represents a type of **involuntary alienation** and involves (1) the process of **condemnation** and (2) **payment of just compensation** to the displaced owner.

In practice, the determination of what constitutes "just compensation" is subject to court battles, and is rarely as simple, or as "just," as it sounds in principle.

Also, condemnation under eminent domain is entirely different from the condemnation of property under safety or health codes.

Escheat is also one of the four government powers. It refers to the transfer of property ownership from an individual to the government when the individual dies **intestate**, or without a will, and **with no known heirs**. The transfer is often phrased as **reverting** to the government.

Escheat also transfers certain types of property to the government at the end of a statutory period of inactivity, as with dormant bank accounts or abandoned property.

Property, such as land or bank accounts, that escheats to the government may be available to be claimed by heirs or owners once they make their interest and legal standing in the property known.

Private Controls on Planning and Zoning (e.g., liens, encumbrances, recording and priorities, subdivision/association rules)

Private controls and restrictions on property include *encumbrances*, like certain *liens*, *easements*, and *encroachments*, as well as *subdivision and association rules*.

Encumbrances are non-ownership interests, monetary and non-monetary, that represent a restriction on the use and/or transfer of real property.

A *lien* is a *monetary encumbrance* that asserts the *lienholder* has a creditor's claim to a specific monetary interest in the property's value. A lien may be satisfied by the property owner through simply paying the debt directly or by paying the debt out of the proceeds of a property sale.

Liens are generally effective the day they are *registered,* or *recorded*, or officially filed, in the appropriate office of public records.

Registering a document provides what is referred to as *constructive notice*, or *legal notice*, which means that a *due diligence* review of the record would make the existence of the document known to the reviewer. This differs from *actual notice*, which means that a party *has personally received the notice*, as when the party has to *sign for the delivery of a document* or *a process server delivers a subpoena* to appear in court.

In the event more than one lien is recorded, the *priority of liens* for payment after a voluntary or forced property sale typically goes by *date of registration* from the first to the most recent. However, the government is a line-jumper, and *property tax liens are always superior to other liens*, regardless of when they became effective.

Mechanic's liens are property liens placed by those that supplied labor or materials for property improvements and went unpaid.

Liens can be categorized as *voluntary*, which means the debt was approved by and acceptable to the owner, such as a mortgage, or *involuntary*, which means they have been placed against the owner's will, such as a tax lien, court judgment, or other claims against a property for equity interest.

Voluntary and involuntary liens may be further classified as being *general*, which affects all of a debtor's property and assets, as in a bankruptcy proceeding or tax lien, or *specific* (or *special*), which means it is limited to a specified item controlled by the debtor, such as a mortgage on a house or loan on a car.

*You may also see references to **statutory** liens, which are created automatically by statute, as with tax liens, and **equitable** liens, which are created by a court order, as in a judgment lien. These distinctions are too specialized for test use except as distractors.*

A short list of common types of liens and their broad categories includes
- *mortgage liens*, which result from property financing, are <u>voluntary, specific</u> liens
- *mechanic's liens*, which result from non-payment of claims by those who worked on a property, are <u>involuntary, specific</u> liens
- *property tax liens*, which result from unpaid taxes, are <u>involuntary, general</u> liens
- *judgment liens*, which result from a court order to pay a certain amount to a creditor, are <u>involuntary, general</u> liens

Non-monetary encumbrances include such physical and legal restrictions as *easements*, *encroachments*, *subdivision restrictions*, and *owners' association rules* that encumber the use and/or transfer of property.

Easements are interests in land that give a nonowner the right to use a property for a specific purpose, generally to cross over it. Easements affording access are commonly distinguished as either *appurtenant* or *in gross*.

An *easement appurtenant*, or *appurtenant easement*, is the right to use one property for the benefit of another one. The most common example is a *right-of-way* across someone else's land to get to one that has no other access. The right to enter, exit, and reenter is sometimes referred to as *ingress*, *egress*, and *regress*, respectively.

An *easement by necessity*, or *easement of necessity*, is a special, but common, type of appurtenant easement that arises automatically in cases where an owner sells a *landlocked parcel* of a larger property.

In these situations, the property that provides, and must allow, the access is referred to as the *servient tenement*, or *servient estate*, since that property is a 'servant' to the interest of the one that requires it. The land that 'commands' the benefits of this use is referred to as the *dominant tenement*, or *dominant estate*.

Appurtenant rights and interests such as those above are said to *run with the land*, which means they typically remain in full force even if omitted from the language of a deed during a property transfer.

Future sales of properties with an easement appurtenant should include clear reference to the easement in all applicable documents to not only clarify the scope and limits of the easement, but to help assert and ensure its continued existence.

An **easement in gross** differs from an easement appurtenant in that **there is only a servient tenement**. For example, a **utilities easement**, or **utilities pass-through**, for sewer pipes and telephone lines do not benefit a utility company's physical property, so there is no neighboring dominant tenement, but **the servient tenement owner must allow access for maintenance and repairs**.

Other common examples of **easements in gross** are **those for personal use**, as when an owner lets a neighbor or friend cross a property as a shortcut or to get to a waterway. Such **personal-use easements** are typically not transferable, and terminate with the death of either party or the sale of the property.

However, owners that allow others to use their land without a specific arrangement may lose the right to stop that use if it becomes protected by law after a legal action for an **easement by prescription**, or **prescriptive easement**.

Prescriptive easements must meet several legal tests, most notably, that the use of the property has occurred regularly for the minimum **statutory period** required by law.

This period of **adverse use**, meaning that **the use may have adverse consequences on the owner's unencumbered property rights**, is **twenty years** in Bermuda for most land uses. *Consult a lawyer for confirmation of applicability regarding specific situations.*

Other conditions for acquiring an easement by prescription include several particulars about the pattern of use. Typically, the use must be characterized as **open**, **notorious**, and **hostile** in the legal meaning of these terms.

*Similar terms arise in different real estate textbook and legal dictionary definitions of prescriptive easements, and perhaps on tests. The following terms may be understood as incorporated into the legal meaning of their closest match above: **visible, continuous, exclusive,** and **adverse**.*

Also, such property use is more likely to entitle the user to an easement by prescription if the owner is unaware through years of neglect than if the owner has knowingly allowed the use to occur.

Some legal authorities recommend posting a sign indicating "use by permission" or "walkers welcome" on a subject property to thwart prescriptive claims by providing open, public notice of permissive use.

In some more public cases, such as when a private entity owns a road or gathering place used by the public, that entity may publish a notice and then block off the private property one day a year to formally assert its continued right to do so.

Prescriptive easements are often confused with adverse possession, which is discussed briefly in the next section under involuntary alienation; with adverse possession of a property, actual title is transferred based on similar claims made to legally acquire a prescriptive easement.

Party wall easements are just what the name suggests: a common building wall or a stand-alone wall either on or at a property line, and therefore involves both owners in ownership, maintenance, and/or access issues.

Creation and termination of easements represents a longer, more detailed list than is worth itemizing here, given their relatively self-evident nature, legal technicalities, and low importance for entry-level testing. However, a few of the most common categories include
- *creation of easements* may arise through
  - ***mutual agreement*** of the parties, either in writing (***express***) or through behavior (***implied***)
  - ***necessity***, as with certain landlocked properties
  - ***longtime use***, as in a prescriptive easement
- *termination of easements* may occur through
  - ***abandonment*** of use
  - ***release of easement*** by the owner of the dominant estate
  - ***conclusion of the reason*** for the easement
  - ***merger of the dominant and servient estates*** through purchase of one property by the owner of the other

A *license* is a personal, revocable right or privilege granted by an owner to someone else to use the property, typically in a brief, limited way. A license, which is often simply a verbal approval, can be seen as changing a trespasser into a visitor. It is ***not considered a type of easement*** and may or may not include compensation. Examples include tickets to use a parking lot, attend an event, or watch a movie in a theater.

Encroachments are a special type of encumbrance that involve ***some form of overlapping use of one property by another***, as when a portion of a building actually crosses the line, known technically as ***trespass***, or tree limbs or a roofline extend across a property boundary, known technically as ***nuisance***.

Whether or not such close calls as those above are encroachments are often resolved by either a ***visual inspection*** or a ***property survey***, which determines ***the accurate location and dimensions of property boundary lines***. Surveys are also used to ***discover unrecognized encroachments***.

Encroachments are legally categorized as *unauthorised and/or illegal infringements that can affect a title's marketability*, but they may arise and exist with the knowledge and consent of the owners.

An encroachment *may affect the marketability of title for both properties* unless it is adequately addressed. Depending on the situation, some simple encroachments may be removed by

- *selling the property* in question to the encroaching property owner
- *deeding the use as an easement*

Another property encumbrance that affects the marketability of a property's title is a *lis pendens*, which is Latin for *"pending lawsuit."*

- If a *lis pendens* has been recorded against the property, it means that *some form of litigation against the property is pending* that *may become the responsibility of a new owner* to address.

Other private restrictions on land use include *subdivision covenants, conditions (or codes), and restrictions*, and *owners' association rules* for most common interest ownership arrangements. These are *non-monetary encumbrances* that encumber the use and/or transfer of property.

Regardless of their label, they generally seek to accomplish similar ends, such as allow or disallow pets in a subdivision or complex, or clarify where to put trash and recyclables. Depending on the property type and local conventions for terminology, they may be referred to as

- *deed restrictions* or *restrictive covenants*
- *condominium owners' association rules* for condominium-specific restrictions
- *homeowners' association rules* for subdivision-specific restrictions

Private restrictions are often more restrictive than local zoning ordinances, which means they may either *enhance or detract from property values*. *Private restrictions* on land use are *contractual rather than statutory* and are prepared by *subdivision developers* as well as *individual property owners* to limit the use of a property by future owners. For example, a *developer* may sell lots with restrictions on building styles or property uses.

I-C. Property Valuation

Principles, Types, and Estimates of Property Value

Principles, types, and estimates of property value are firmly grounded in the many concepts, terms, and processes that constitute the professional practice of appraisers yet are also used daily by real estate licensees.

I. Principles and Practices of Real Estate   (40 questions)

For testing purposes, the emphasis of the questions will be on how real estate licensees apply and explain the following principles and valuation/appraisal methods. In fact, most of the questions are written to identify how a licensee, not an appraiser, uses them. So even though the following has a lot of appraiser-type information, <u>you</u> will be using it, too!

Test questions, though, that concentrate on what an appraiser does will use that term. Since the valuation practices of real estate licensees should be patterned on professional appraisal principles and methods, this is not inappropriate: your valuation estimates—and your explanations of them to clients—should strive to match those of a good appraiser.

Principles of property value used by appraisers and real estate licensees alike include the principles of
- **substitution**, which looks at the maximum amount it would **cost to buy an alternate property** that is the same as the subject property, **either by a comparable replacement or an exact reproduction**; this principle is central to two of **the three approaches to value** described later in this Topic Area
- **anticipation**, which estimates value based on **looking ahead at the value, positive or negative**, on a property **due to possibility of future changes** to either the property or its surroundings; this principle is used in the third of three main approaches to value
- **highest and best use**, which determines **the use that will produce the greatest current value, or the most profitable return on investment**, as exemplified by a developer converting a vacant urban industrial building into a profitable residential condo
- **balance**, which refers to **the mix of land uses that maximizes value** for all of the properties involved, as when the proportion of residential, commercial, recreational, industrial, and other uses make **a general area or building complex** attractive to both residents and businesses
- **supply and demand**, which simply applies this common economic principle to real estate. It can be readily seen by considering the amount of competition and prices for an acre of land in central Manhattan versus an acre of land in many Southwestern desert areas
- **competition**, which means that **if a particular property is yielding high profits, similar ones are likely to follow** and try to get in on the action
- **conformity**, which means that all **properties in a given area are likely to benefit from being similar to the others,** as in a subdivision of new homes. When conformity is ignored, it can affect property values in either of the following directions
  - **progression**, which is the **benefit a smaller property receives in increased value** from being among larger, more valuable ones; *unfortunately, increased values from progression may backfire on current owners through tax increases*
  - **regression**, which is the **negative impact on the value of a large and/or more expensive property** when it is in an area of smaller or lower-priced properties
- **contribution**, or **increasing and diminishing returns**, which makes a cost/benefit analysis of **the actual increase in property value based on the cost of an improvement**, as in how much more a house will sell for after a $10,000 kitchen renovation. If the $10,000 kitchen only adds $3,000 to the property's market value, it would be considered an **overimprovement**.
- **depreciation**, which in property valuation refers to **the loss of value resulting from any cause**. Two key terms associated with depreciation are

- *deterioration*, which applies to *physical factors*, such as normal *wear and tear* as well as poor and/or *deferred maintenance*, or *prolonged neglect*
- *obsolescence*, which applies to *outdated functionality* or *non-property influences*

The *three types of depreciation* used in valuations/appraisals, plus whether or not they are *curable*, meaning they can be remedied, or *incurable*, meaning they are not cost-effective or feasible to fix, are

- *physical deterioration,* which refers to *any downturn from the original condition* of the property, such as an old roof, weathered paint, or broken windows
    - *curable* physical deterioration includes *economically feasible repairs*, such as a new exterior paint job
    - *incurable* physical deterioration includes *excessive, cost-prohibitive repairs*, such as correcting a seriously damaged foundation after a landslide or other natural disaster
- *functional obsolescence*, which refers to *outdated design or safety standards*, such as a two-story, three-bedroom house built in the 1920's that still has it original wiring and a single bathroom on the first floor
    - *curable* functional obsolescence would generally include wiring upgrades and new plumbing in the house noted above
    - *incurable* functional obsolescence is generally identified after *weighing the value added* to the property *against the cost of any upgrades and finding the "cure" cost-prohibitive*, sometimes even in comparison to tearing down a building and starting over altogether
- *external obsolescence*, or *economic obsolescence*, or *locational obsolescence*, which refers to *surrounding influences on a subject property*, such as the discovery that a nearby factory has contaminated the groundwater supply
    Style note: *for clarity, test questions often refer to this as **external (economic) obsolescence**.*
    - *curable* external obsolescence – <u>*no such thing*</u>, since it arises from factors "external" to the owner's direct control, and someone else must cure it
    - *incurable* external obsolescence *is the only kind*, since *spending money on the subject property cannot remedy or "cure" the actual problem*

For valuation purposes, *only improvements can be depreciated*. *Land simply loses value*, and even when it does lose value, as it typically does when the property suffers from external (economic) obsolescence, in the process of determining overall property value, *this loss is categorized separately from the losses of depreciated improvements*.

Types of property value are numerous and complicated, since *value* is a broad term for the monetary worth or price of something, or whatever else it might bring in exchange.

Types of property value include the following major categories

- *market value*, or *fair market value*, which is best understood in real estate to mean *the most probable price a property would bring in a competitive, fair, and open market*, in other words, the *price an informed seller is willing to accept* and *an informed buyer is willing to pay*

- *appraised value* is generally intended to *estimate market value*
- *assessed value*, which means *the value a taxing authority has placed on a property* for purposes of tax computations, and *NOT a current, actual market value*, *even if the taxing authority printouts label something "Fair Market Value"*

  In Bermuda, this is known as annual rental value (ARV); see VI-C for more.
- *loan value*, or *mortgage value*, which is the maximum amount a lender will lend
- *insurable value*, which is the maximum amount an insurance company will insure
- *insured value*, or *agreed value*, which is generally the face value of an insurance policy coverage
- *actual cash value*, which is an insurance determination of the *depreciated value* of a property, or *replacement cost minus accrued depreciation*
- *condemnation value*, which identifies what the property is worth to the condemning authority *in an eminent domain proceeding*
- *estate value*, which is the value given on the probated asset list for the real property of a deceased owner

All property values include some commonly understood *elements of value*, which are
- *utility*, which means that it is useful for something
- *scarcity*, which refers to the available supply
- *demand*, which is a combination of *the desire to own it* and *the ability to purchase it*
- *transferability*, which means that *it can be sold or exchanged*

Further, the term *"value"* is *not directly interchangeable* with either *price* or *cost*, since circumstances may create significant differences. For example, the *cost* of a $20,000 addition to a house generally does not add the same amount of resale *value* to the property.

Similarly, the *market price*, which is *the price a property actually sells for*, *may vary considerably from* its *appraised value* or *market value* depending on factors an appraisal does not consider, such as *the motivation of either party to depart from an estimate of fair market value*.

For example, an owner might sell a property for considerably less than market value to a family member, or a buyer may pay more for sentimental or impulsive reasons.

Estimates of property value are all derived from appraisal methods that follow the basic *appraisal process*, which can be defined as an orderly, concise, and systematic procedure for reaching an *estimate of value*.

In fact, according to longstanding appraisal standards, *the most basic definition of an appraisal* is simply *an estimate of value*.

Generally speaking, people commonly "appraise" a property's value while simply driving by, by tossing off remarks like, "That place could go for a million bucks, easy."

However, within the real estate profession, a Bermuda licensee learns how to perform a closer review and prepare an **Opinion of Value**, commonly known elsewhere as a **competitive market analysis (CMA)**, based on the professional appraisal methods and principles sketched in this Topic Area; the Opinion would provide a more probable estimate of a property's value than the simple drive-by.

Formal, full appraisals are generally prepared by a licensed appraiser rather than by a real estate licensee. So, the term "appraiser" will be used in this book when referring to appraisals and the appraisal process and "licensee" will be used when referring to the party preparing Opinions or noting other differences between an Opinion and an appraisal.

The **purpose of an appraisal** is, in most cases, to provide **an estimate** of a property's specific type of value **as of a specified date**, which may differ from the date of the report, that will in turn **support the use intended by the person who ordered the appraisal**.

Since the value of a property can change suddenly and dramatically due to disasters, accidents, or other events, **the appraisal value**, though generally unaffected for some time, **cannot be guaranteed as accurate for any other time than the specified effective date**.

In the course of a full-scope appraisal, an appraiser will analyze a property based on considering each of **three approaches to value**, though only one will have primary applicability to determining the final appraisal value of any particular property.

The three approaches are the **direct sales comparison (market data) approach**, the **cost approach**, and the **income approach**. *Each one will be laid out after the following basic elements of the appraisal process and principles are covered.*

The **appraisal process** can be defined as an **orderly, concise, and systematic procedure for reaching an estimate of value**. It generally follows a common sequence of procedures, which can be summarized by the following check-list
- **define, or state, the problem**, which means clarifying the purpose and scope of the appraisal
- **determine the data needed** and **collect it**
- **determine the highest and best use** of the land and the improvements
- **estimate the property value** using the three approaches to value
- **reconcile the data**, which means to analyze it and settle on a final value estimate
- **prepare the final report** of the value estimate

The **appraisal report** prepared in the final step of the process will follow a format appropriate to the purpose of the report, from a detailed narrative to a simple two-page Uniform Residential Appraisal Report.

Regardless of length, the report will present, analyze, and summarize the data supporting the appraiser's *reconciliation* of data and *final determination-of-value estimate*.

Unfortunately, the definition of an appraisal does not adequately distinguish between a licensee's *Opinion of Value* and an *appraisal* performed by a professional appraiser, since they both provide estimates of value.

The following descriptions identify the primary differences between these two estimates

- a licensee's Opinion of Value, is typically used to establish a *reasonable listing price* for sellers and a *reasonable offering price* for buyers. They generally *analyze the property according to the most applicable of the three approaches to value* presented below, and then, ultimately, after reviewing the Opinion estimate, *it is the seller's responsibility to set a list price* and *the buyer's responsibility to determine an offering price.*
- an appraiser's appraisal is performed by a qualified appraiser and is a *more extensive analysis* that *follows a set of guidelines* by the *Royal Institution of Chartered Surveyors (RICS)* and results in one of several standard-format *appraisal reports*.
  - These generally more rigorously researched reports are typically *required by lenders or insurers* to *support the accuracy and legal accountability of the actual risk they are assuming*.

So, while a licensee's Opinion of Value and an appraiser's appraisal often provide similar estimates of value, the *formal appraisal* provides *stronger documentation* in support of its figure.

*In fact, after widespread—often fraudulent—overvaluation of real estate across the United States in the mid-to-late 1980s lead to bank failures nationwide, the federal government mandated the establishment of professional standards and licensing for appraisers. **The US government still requires lenders** making certain **federally backed residential loans** to support their values **with an appraisal by a licensed appraiser**.*

The licensee's Opinion of Value is still useful, and usually acceptably accurate, in estimating property value, typically since most follow the methods of appraisal analyses.

Estimates of property value, according to appraisal standards, requires an analysis of a property based on each of the following *three approaches to value*; typically, though, only one will have primary applicability to any particular property.

The *first approach*, the *direct sales comparison (market data) approach*, generally referred to in Bermuda simply as the *sales comparison* or *sales comparable* approach, compares the *subject property*, or *subject*, which is the one being appraised, to similar properties, or *comparable properties*, or *comparables*, or "*comps*," that have recently sold in the local market.

*Style note: the above term for this approach is a common testing convention, since it combines the terms **direct sales comparison**, **sales comparison**, and **market data**.*

This comparison is used to estimate the subject property's **relative value in the same market** that produced the sale of the comparables. This means that **the sale of a comparable must be fair and open market sale** rather than a forced or insider sale.

This approach to value is **an application of the principle of substitution**, since it assumes that similar properties are similarly desirable and may be substituted for each other. It is widely and **extensively used for residential properties**.

When available, **three or more comparables are reviewed** and analyzed to provide a balanced estimate.

The **price of a comparable gets adjusted up or down** based on valuable differences between it and the subject property – **the final figure is applied to the subject**.

For example, if the subject and the comparable houses **were identical except one has an extra bay in its garage**, the value of the extra bay would be used to adjust for price comparisons.
- **If the comparable has the extra bay**, the bay's value would be **subtracted from its sales price** to estimate the market value of the subject property.
- **If the subject property has the bay**, its value would be **added to the comparable's sales price** to estimate the market value of the subject.

All relevant property conditions, including influences from **depreciation**, are factored into the final estimate of value using the direct sales comparison (market data) approach.

The **second approach**, the **cost approach**, estimates value based on **what it would cost to buy the land and build comparable replacements** for all of the property improvements.

The **cost approach is based on the principle of substitution**, since it assumes that no rational person will pay more for a property than the amount it would cost to purchase a comparable site and construct a comparable building without any undue delays.

The cost approach is commonly **used for commercial properties, as well as for special-use properties** that do not have many comparables, such as **churches, schools, and municipal buildings**.

In order to adjust for the difference between new construction and existing improvements, the **current structures are evaluated for depreciation, which is then subtracted from the new construction cost**.

There are **five steps** in the preparation of a cost approach analysis. These are
- **estimate the value of the land only**, as if vacant
- **estimate the new construction cost** of all improvements

- *determine the accrued, or combined, depreciation* from the three types of depreciation as they affect the current improvements
- *subtract the accrued depreciation* of the improvements from the estimate of new construction to get the estimated value of the current improvements
- *add the value of the land to the value of the improvements*

The completion of the last step will produce the *estimated property value by the cost approach*.

The primary method for *determining the new construction costs* of improvements needed for the steps above is known as the *replacement cost*.

- *Replacement cost* determines *the current cost of an acceptably similar copy*, often somewhat more contemporary in functionality and construction.

  There are several ways to estimate the above construction costs, including the *square-foot method*, the *unit-in-place method*, the *quantity survey method*, and the *index method*. Details of these methods are best left to appraiser exams.

  However, the *square-foot method* is so commonly used in practice for estimating a wide variety of new-construction that it may appear in math questions.

  To compute construction costs using the square-foot method, simply *multiply the cost-per-square-foot of building a comparable property by the square footage of a new building*.

  So, if a 10,000 square foot warehouse were built for $397,500, or $39.75/square foot, a 12,000 square foot warehouse would cost $477,000.

The *third approach*, the *income approach*, estimates the present value of future net income of income-producing properties through the process of *capitalization*, which converts *future income projections into current value*.

The *income approach is generally the most applicable when analyzing investment properties*, such as retail, commercial, industrial, and residential rental properties.

Using *the income approach*, a licensee would estimate the present value of future net income of income-producing properties through the process of *capitalization*, which converts *future income projections into current value*.

The *income approach* is *based on the principle of anticipation*, which asserts that value is created by the expectation of benefits to be derived from *return on investment* during ownership as well as any capital gain realized at resale.

The *capitalization rate*, or *cap rate*, is the term for the *rate of return* on the cost of the investment.

To *compute the capitalization rate* for a particular property, simply *divide the property's net operating income (NOI) by its price*.

- For example, a $2,000,000 property that has a $200,000/year NOI has a capitalization rate of 10 percent.

The following *three categories of income* are important to remember for rentals and other investment properties. (All of these will be repeated and used in I-H, Property Management.) *The last of these is the one to use for computing cap rates.*

- *potential gross income*, or *projected gross income*, or *scheduled gross income*, which means the *maximum rental income* at 100 percent occupancy
- *effective gross income*, which means the *actual income* after subtracting vacancies and rent collection losses
- *net operating income (NOI)*, which is *what's left of the effective gross income after subtracting all of the property's operating expenses*, such as maintenance, taxes, insurance, reserves for replacements, and other recurring expenses (*but not debt service*, such as mortgage interest)

To *estimate a property value from a cap rate*, an appraiser, licensee, or investor may analyze several recent comparable sales to determine their cap rates, develop an appropriate composite cap rate for the subject property, then *divide the subject property's NOI by the cap rate*.

- For example, if an analysis determines that a cap rate of 5 percent is what the area market is currently supporting, and the NOI for a property is $100,000, the estimated property value would be $2,000,000.

The *gross rent multiplier (GRM)*, or *gross income multiplier (GIM)* method of estimating value is a simple, informal rule-of-thumb technique that is often used for one-to-four unit residential rentals or small commercial and industrial sites.

Using recent sales, the appraiser, licensee, or investor *divides each comparable property's sales price by its gross income, either monthly or annual*, using the same time-period standard for all, to determine their respective GRMs.

Then, after developing a representative GRM from a reconciliation of the collective GRMs, the appraiser, licensee, or investor *multiplies the subject property's income by the GRM* to arrive at a general estimate of value.

For example, if the appraiser, licensee, or investor develops a GRM of 135 for monthly rents in an area, and is analyzing a property with a monthly rent of $1,200, the property's value would be expected to be around $162,000.

In practice, the income approach is very ₛₑₙₛᵢₜᵢᵥₑ to property differences and complexities, highly specialized analysis techniques, and disagreements among appraisers about applications.

The above explanation is intentionally very basic, and is presented more to expose you to a few terms you may see on the test than to provide a short-course in income approach appraisal methods.

Ultimately, a licensee's role in preparing a CMA involves **gathering, interpreting, and computing the value of comparable properties** as well as performing other **property-related math**. Therefore, some of the appraisal topics raised above are directly applicable to test questions.

Additional Valuation and Investment Considerations

Valuation and investment issues for each of the three approaches to value include basic elements regarding the costs and benefits of ownership and property transfers, such as recognizing **general influences on property values** as well as analyzing the **tax implications of ownership and financing**, and **cost/benefit projections for income properties**.

Other **general influences** on property value include applications of the principles of value identified throughout this Topic Area, often in combination with other considerations, such as **overall market conditions**, which take into account **the economic climate and the supply of properties that are in demand**.

The real estate adage that "the three most important considerations in property value are location, location, and location" leads us to list some of the factors that make location so important. Among them are national, regional, local, and neighborhood considerations of

- *economic circumstances*, which include elements such as
  - local business and employment opportunities
  - availability of private utilities, such as phone service and cable
- *government controls, regulations, and services*, such as
  - taxation
  - zoning restrictions
  - anticipation of the exercise of eminent domain/compulsory purchase
  - availability of public utilities
  - schools and other municipal services
- *environmental conditions*, such as
  - annual weather patterns
  - natural resources, such as mountains, lakes, or seashore
  - topographical elements, such as soil types and wetlands, swamp, or desert
  - possible hazards, such as hurricanes, flooding, or mudslides
  - recreation areas and outlets
  - local industries and potential air, soil, and water pollution
- *social trends*, such as
  - region and municipality demographic makeup
  - neighborhood cycles and population changes

Property-specific considerations are generally at the center of all value considerations. Some of the property-specific factors to consider may include, but are not limited to

- *overall condition*, such as whether it is new construction or a "handyman special"
  - *property depreciation is a critical term associated with property condition and value; remember, it is defined as the loss of value resulting from any cause*
- *construction type*, meaning both design style and materials
- *amenities*, which could be *internal*, such as an indoor Jacuzzi, *or external*, such as a better view of some attractive sight than the neighboring properties offer
- *site improvements*, such as outbuildings, wells, or connections to public utilities
- *defects*, such as structural problems or negative actions of past owners that have made it a *stigmatized property*, or *psychologically impacted property*
- *historic value*, if any, such as being on the Bermuda National Trust list or being near a National Trust listed historic site
- *aesthetic factors*, such as a unique architectural design, attractive appearance, or "curb appeal"
- *distance from population centers, work, shopping, and major roads*

Questions from this Topic Area will include **appraisal-type questions***, but often* **from the perspective of a licensee who is preparing an Opinion of Value***; watch for the use of "licensee," "agent," or "broker" rather than "appraiser" in such questions.*

Some of the property conditions that might be used in these examples include

- *general property information* for the listing, such as age, condition, or zoning
- *material defects*, which are defects that would affect a potential buyer's decision on either buying the property or how much to pay
- *internal environmental problems*, such as the existence of asbestos or toxic mold
- *external environmental problems*, such as soil contamination or air pollution
- *stigmatizing conditions*, or *psychologically impacted properties*, such as a history of illegal activity or health information about a seller or past residents
- *adjustments to comparable properties*, such as extra amenities and features that make the subject property different from particular comps
- *depreciation considerations* as they apply to the subject property's final value

MATH Questions!!

Before moving on, it is worth noting there are likely to be *between two and four math questions* from all of this Topic Area. The questions will provide all the numbers and information necessary to do the math.

The topics are most likely to concentrate on exploring valuation considerations that a licensee *might reasonably need to compute to support figures on a CMA, explain an appraisal report's figures, or justify the amount of an offer to purchase.*

These would include, but not be limited to, the following situations

- *determining list price* from data related to one of the three approaches to value
- *depreciation computations* based on depreciation data provided in the question
- *making adjustments* to the comparable property's sales price
- *determining the price of a subject property* from data on comparables
- *computing replacement or reproduction cost* given the necessary price information
- *investment projections* for income properties
- *determining the final sales price* from broker's commission information

SPECIAL MATH TIPS:

- *Most of the math questions on the test are not particularly complicated. Those that are simply require you to take a deep breath and think a little harder. Chances are that you will be able to at least rule out a few of the answer choices and then be able to make a better-odds guess at whatever's left.*
- *ANSWER EVERY QUESTION – an unanswered question is guaranteed to count against you; a guess has a 25% chance of being another point for you.*
- *For those of you with math anxiety, one strategy for tackling them is to make a small mark next to the question number for each math question on your answer sheet, leaving the answer itself blank, then move on immediately to the next question.*
    - *After answering all of the <u>non-math</u> questions, you can then return to <u>JUST</u> the math questions and work them as a group, doing the ones that look easiest first.*
    - *Remember the following point, and then relax: you can do poorly on the math and still pass the exam with room to spare if you get enough of the non-math questions right!*

I-D. Contracts (e.g., basic contract law, listings, sales, leases, options)

Basic Contract Law

This area of real estate relies directly on *basic contract law* for its technical understanding of commonly *required elements*, terms for *types of contracts*, and other basic *contract terminology*, including *contract provisions*, *contingencies*, and *termination* or *breach* issues.

The specific *basic, required elements of a valid contrac*t may vary slightly depending on what kind of contract it is. They may also appear, as is so common in legal language, under interchangeable terms.

Some of the following terms will be further addressed in areas where they have more common applications. However, these elements are commonly identified as

- *legally competent parties*, which means they have *legal capacity* to enter into contracts. This usually *excludes* legal minors and those judged mentally incompetent.
- *offer and acceptance*, also known as a *meeting of the minds*, or *mutual assent*, which means that something is being offered by one party and accepted without qualification by the other
- *consideration*, which means the payment or promise of something of value, generally money, in exchange for what has been offered

- *legal purpose,* or *legality of object*, which means that *the contract is not for an illegal purpose*, such as disposing of toxic waste in an undeveloped residential subdivision, or a house rental in which illegal drugs will be produced
- *reality of consent*, which means that *both parties acted under their own free will*, without *duress*, and that all of the information they had at hand on which to base their decision was accurate and adequate

Other elements that may be required, depending on the contract, include that it
- *be in writing* if required by the *statute of frauds* or other applicable laws for commercial exchanges
    - the *statute of frauds* is a common law statute that has been specifically adopted by many jurisdictions and requires contracts for the *sale or transfer of interest in real estate* or real estate *rentals for <u>more than</u> one year* to be *in writing in order to be enforceable in court*
        > *Bermuda's Conveyancing Act 1983 extends this common law period for oral leases to THREE YEARS; it also requires contracts for the disposition of land to be in writing.*
- *include all signatures of parties* required to sign, for example, the grantor of a deed
- *give an adequate description of the property* as required for various real estate listing, sales, and mortgage contracts as well as deeds; street addresses may be acceptable for listings and rentals, whereas *an adequate legal description is required for deeds*

Types of contracts involve *basic contract terminology* that includes a host of *opposite pairings* with specific legal interpretations; these contract terms address the most basic nature of real estate contracts, which begins with *whether or not a contract exists*, and if so, *upon which parties it is binding*. For example
- a *valid* contract refers to one that includes *certain critical elements* (noted above) and so has full legal force and effect
    - an *invalid* contract *lacks at least one of those critical elements*, and is therefore either void or voidable
- a *void* contract is one that has no legal force due to its *lack of one or more elements* required for validity, and can be said to not be a contract at all
    - a *voidable* contract is seen as binding on one party but not on the other, who is free to pursue it or 'void' it
- a *unilateral*, or *'one-sided,'* contract is one in which only one party has made a promise to do something, such as offering a reward to the person who finds a lost pet
    - a *bilateral*, or *'two-sided,'* contract is one in which both parties have made a promise and are obligated to follow through on all of the contract's conditions or risk being in breach of contract
- an *enforceable* contract is one that meets the legal requirements for validity, and therefore requires all parties to observe their contractual obligations

- an *unenforceable* contract may be either a void contract or one that was valid when made but legally unenforceable due to some technical fine point, such as the destruction of an unrecorded deed
- an *express* contract generally means that the understanding has been explicitly set out, *typically in writing, though it could be oral*
  - an *implied* contract generally refers to *the conduct* of the parties providing sufficient indication that they have a common understanding

Further, when parties enter into a contract and proceed to satisfy its conditions, the following contract terminology applies

- the term *execute*, as a verb, means *both*
  1. *to sign a contract* as well as
  2. *to fulfill and complete the contract's conditions*.
     When used in the latter sense, an *executed contract* may also be termed *fully performed*, or *discharged*.
- the term *executory* refers to a contract that is *in the process of being fulfilled*

Listing Contracts

A *listing contract*, or *listing agreement*, is a contract that engages a real estate licensee's firm to market a property in exchange for receiving compensation, usually in the form of a commission, upon the sale and transfer of the property.

A licensee's disclosure and explanation of agency relationships to a principal includes explaining that since a licensee acts as a general agent for their "employing" agent, *when a licensee takes a listing, the licensee is actually creating an agency relationship between the principal and the broker/brokerage firm; the licensee's relationship is as subagent of the brokerage's broker.*

This is the most logical place to note this important point about the creation of agency relationships; however, more specific coverage on all this will come in Section II—Law of Agency.

*Also, in a close, legal interpretation of agency relationships, it can be argued that because the agency relationship created by listing contracts is between the principal and the licensee's broker/brokerage firm, **the listing licensee** is not a fiduciary for the principal—that's the position of the broker/brokerage firm—but **does owe fiduciary duties to the principal on behalf of the broker/brokerage firm.***

*These distinctions are legally too refined for testing, but are mentioned here to help address the finer distinctions that are commonly left unexplained in textbooks. They may also help you understand **the basic legal right brokerages have for retaining listings when listing licensees leave the firm**, or even the authority to transfer listings to another licensee, such as if the principal becomes dissatisfied with the listing licensee.*

The most common types of listing agreements are

- *sole listing,* or *exclusive right to sell*, which engages a single agency to market the property and entitles that agency to a full commission regardless of who finds the buyer, even if it is the property owner; *this type of listing agreement provides the greatest protection for the licensee to collect compensation*

- *exclusive listing,* or *exclusive agency*, which engages a single agency to market the property and entitles that agency to a commission if anyone *other than* the property owner finds the buyer; *though **this type of listing is not currently in common use in Bermuda**, it is mentioned here to illustrate this method for structuring an agency relationship that falls between sole/exclusive and open/nonexclusive*

- *open*, or *nonexclusive*, which allows the property owner to engage any number of agencies to market the property, and only entitles the agency that procures the buyer to a commission; if the property owner finds the buyer, none of the agencies or licensees are entitled to any compensation

- *net*, which engages an agency to market a property and receive as compensation all sale proceeds in excess of the owner's stated "net" for the property, or amount over a list price

  - *In Bermuda, net listings are prohibited under the **Real Estate Brokers' Licensing Act 2017**; there is more on this subject in Topic Areas V-C, Remuneration, and V-G, Listings.*

    - *They are defined here, and tested, because they represent a way of structuring a listing agreement and compensation.*

    - *Nevertheless, **they are widely viewed as unethical** due to their potential for creating a licensee conflict of interest, or **even allowing direct exploitation** of an unsophisticated seller, **which is why they are illegal in Bermuda.***

Listing agreement contracts, like all contracts, *require some very specific elements* for their validity. In addition, though, they may contain a host of other components that address common practice, terms, and conventions in a particular market area or state.

To create a valid listing agreement, the following elements need to be added to the basic elements necessary for a valid contract given above

- *required signatures* includes *all* of the owners and the listing licensee
- *property description* sufficient to identify the property; it need not be the legal description required on a deed
- *list price* of the property
- *definite termination/expiration date*, which ensures that a property owner does not get locked into an arrangement that the owner has to actively terminate

  *In Bermuda, this requirement **does NOT currently apply to open listings, though it does to exclusive agreements, i.e. both sole and exclusive listings**; see Topic Area V-G, Listings, for more.*

- *agent compensation*, which describes when it is earned and how it is computed.

Agency employment contract is an increasingly widespread way *to describe time-honored listing agreements*, as well as other, newer representation arrangements, in order to clarify their *status as employment contracts that specify the licensee's duties, obligations, agency relationship, and compensation arrangements.*

> *Agency relationships and local terminology have been the subject of great discussion and jurisdiction-specific legislation for over twenty years. See below, II, Law of Agency, for a broad treatment of agency relationships.*

A *buyer agency agreement* is a contract that engages a real estate licensee to search for suitable property on behalf of a potential buyer in exchange for receiving compensation, usually in the form of a commission, upon the purchase and transfer of the property.

> In these arrangements the licensee is often referred to as a *buyer's broker* when representing only the buyer.

Listing contracts, like many other agreements, *may be terminated*, or *cancelled*, for an assortment of reasons, including

- *completion* of the transaction through *performance*, or *fulfillment*, of contract elements
- *expiration* of the contract period
- *mutual agreement* of the parties
- *breach of contract* by one of the parties, which generally incurs liability for the party in breach
- *lack of legal elements* in the original contract, such as finding that the contract was made for an illegal purpose
- *bankruptcy* of either party
- *destruction* of the property
- *death or incapacity* of a party
- *abandonment of agency services* by the agent, which may make the agent liable for breach of contract
- *condemnation* of the property under an eminent domain/compulsory purchase action

Compensation Agreements

Compensation agreements refer to a host of creative compensation arrangements, including the traditional commission percentage arrangement.

> Nevertheless, a *commission-based compensation agreement* of any kind typically identifies the *commission percentage* rate based on the gross sales price, who is entitled to collect, and *commission-splitting* arrangements for *cooperating agents*.

> However, *compensation arrangements in a buyer agency agreement* can be complicated by whether or not the buyer pays the agent directly for specific assistance in locating and securing a property or allows the agent to collect a listed property's commission split.

Plus there has been a recent rise in **companies offering to help market property** under some form of **flat-fee for limited services**, often just signs, property information flyers, and a posting in a multiple listing service (MLS), rather than charging a conventional commission for conventional full-service marketing. Some such companies set charges based on a list of **fees-for-services** plus **reimbursements** for certain marketing expenses.

> NOTE: **Bermuda** *may not have comparable* **antitrust**, *or* **business monopoly**, *laws on the books to those mentioned below, but the terms and concepts are nevertheless widely applicable. Also, certain antitrust violations as identified herein may be actionable in Bermuda as a breach of business ethics or an unfair business practice, so pay attention!*
>
> **Guidelines to acceptable industry practices for setting real estate fees may be found in the Bermuda Chamber of Commerce's Real Estate Division's <u>Real Estate Handbook</u>.**

An **important consideration** in setting commissions and compensation arrangements has to do with **avoiding antitrust violations** by **maintaining open market competition** rather than **agreeing with competitors to standardize rates and fees**.

The following compensation arrangements also invite scrutiny for their basic ethical nature and legality under antitrust laws, especially when they are undisclosed.

- **referral fees**, which are fees earned by referring business to someone, and may be seen as a violation of antitrust laws if they are related to a tie-in agreement; *however, many types of referral fees are acceptable in Bermuda by other licensed real estate brokers*
- **kickbacks**, which means the return of a portion of a payment received by a vendor to another individual involved in the vendor's getting some business, especially when it is part of a secret agreement. Like a referral fee, it may be a violation of antitrust laws if it is part of a tie-in agreement.

The best way to handle these situations is to avoid them. The next-best way to handle **any compensation payments to or from anyone**, be it a commission, referral fee, gift, bonus, "finder's fee" to unlicensed parties, or anything else of value, is to **get the written, informed consent of all parties** to the transaction. This practice **may not be a specific legal or company requirement,** but is a good safeguard against basic misunderstandings and financial disputes anywhere.

Compensation disputes often arise in cases where a licensee introduces a party to a property and then that party either buys through another licensee or finds a way to deal directly with the owner.

These disputes are legally resolved based on the application of the concept of **procuring cause**, which refers to determining if a licensee's efforts were instrumental in leading to the sale of real estate and is therefore generally entitled to a commission.

> **Bermuda** *law covers this concept in the* **Real Estate Brokers' Licensing Act 2017**; *see Topic Area V-C,* **Remuneration***, for more.*

The traditional test for procuring cause, and arguable entitlement for an earned commission, is finding a buyer who is **ready, willing, and able to meet the seller's terms**.

In some jurisdictions this is determined by who introduced the buyer to a property, regardless of who actually writes the offers and counteroffers for the buyer.

Also, in many jurisdictions, finding a ready, willing, and able buyer who meets the seller's terms is all that is required for a licensee to be entitled to a commission. In those jurisdictions, if the seller backs out of a contract, or refuses to accept an offer that meets the listing specifications, the licensee may be able to successfully sue for compensation.

Further, many jurisdictions allow various forms of protection for licensees in the event a principal acts unethically by telling the other party to wait until after the agency agreement period expires and then return as a "free" party to pursue the transaction without having to incur a sales commission.

*Commonly known as **broker protection clauses**, they may be written into agency employment contracts/listings using language that reinforces the broker's right to collect a commission for particular sales that occur even after contract termination.*

Sales Contracts

The paperwork and documentation trail in real estate sales transaction progresses from listing a property to **offers**, **counteroffers**, and **sales contracts**.

Offers, like so many other real estate terms, may have a locally 'correct' label, such as **offer to purchase**, **offer to purchase and contract**, and similar terms. The purpose of an offer is **to set forth the conditions the prospective buyer proposes to the seller**.

But **an offer is not a contract**, since the offeree has not accepted it; **it may, though, become a contract upon acceptance of all of its conditions by the offeree**.

A **counteroffer** is the common term for the offer **if the offeree** makes **a change of any kind to it and returns it to the original offeror.** The following principles apply to offers and counteroffers
- **any change** to the original offer legally **terminates that offer** and indicates the original has been **rejected and replaced** by the updated offer; the same is true of a counteroffer
- **changes to offers and counteroffers should be initialed by all principals**
- an offer, or counteroffer, can be **revoked by the offeror** at **any time prior to its acceptance**
- **the offeree may cancel**, or **nullify**, the offer simply **by letting the response period expire** without responding.

Submission of offers and counteroffers is commonly understood to mean that *a licensee working for a principal is responsible for submitting all offers*, regardless of the terms offered or whether the property is already under contract.

Further, even when the principal has instructed a licensee not to present offers of a certain type or from certain parties, the licensee is commonly expected to inform the principal of all offers.

Some of the questions in this area may be scenario-type that serve to illustrate the above point of **submitting all offers**, *not just the best, or those over a particular amount, or with certain conditions, but* **all** *offers*.

Other aspects of submitting offers, such as the legality of e-mail correspondence, fax transmissions, or oral binders, are not uniformly recognized or applied, so are unlikely to be tested on the general exam.

Earnest money is the term for the *deposit*, or *down payment*, that *accompanies an offer* to purchase real estate; it *demonstrates the buyer's good-faith, "earnest" intention to complete the transaction and supply the balance* of *the full offer price*, or *consideration*, *at closing*.

If the contract includes a *liquidated damages provision*, earnest money may also provide a source of funds *for damages to the seller in the event of buyer default*.

Both the use and the amount of earnest money are governed more by convention than law; *earnest money does not constitute "consideration" and is not a legal requirement for creating a binding sales contract*. However, most offers are accompanied by *some* earnest money, and *a buyer's seriousness of purpose* is commonly seen in direct proportion to the size of the earnest money check.

These and other critical earnest money considerations, such as *how much a buyer provides, conditions of its use and/or return* in the event of offer rejection or sales contract termination, and *liquidated damages provisions* are *all subject to negotiation between the parties*.

Once an offer or counteroffer has become a mutually accepted and binding contract, it is variously known as a *purchase agreement*, a *purchase contract*, a *sales contract*, a *purchase and sale contract*, an *agreement for sale*, or another similar term.

A *properly executed purchase agreement* identifies the specific property, sets out all of the contractual requirements for its transfer from one party to another, and *generally serves as the complete agreement between parties*.

As previously noted, *offer and acceptance* is a requirement of a valid contract, and is generally the final element needed for a valid real estate sales contract.

I. Principles and Practices of Real Estate   (40 questions)

Contract **provisions** refer to the particular information, conditions, and instructions provided in the contract that govern the many details that have to be addressed in **the 'performance'** of the contract.

Provisions are too numerous to list, or test, in detail, but include commonplace elements like
- **personal property included**, which specifies what stays, like firewood or appliances *(**Ownership of personal property** is legally transferred at closing through a **bill of sale**, which will trump all other options in a test question on this point.)*
- **time is of the essence clause**, which serves to underline and **reinforce the importance of meeting contract dates**, and that **failure to do so will be considered a contract breach and grounds for cancellation of the contract**
- **option**, which is most often in a **commercial property purchase offer** and serves to hold a property open for a specified period at a specified price **in exchange for some monetary consideration**, which is **generally (1) applied toward the purchase price** if all of the conditions are met and the sale goes through, **or (2) kept by the owner if there is no sale**.
  - An **option is a type of unilateral contract**, which is **binding on the seller to sell, but not on the buyer to buy**.
  - A **lease-option**, or **lease with an option to buy**, is a mixture of a lease and a purchase contract, but begins as **a lease with a clause allowing the tenant to exercise an option to purchase the property**. *Lease-options are presented here for comparison with option contracts for purchases; the lease-option definition will be repeated later in this Topic Area under Leases.*
- **"as is"** refers to the property being sold in its existing condition without guarantees for its physical condition or title; **this provision generally does not protect a seller from liability for known material defects**
- **"subject to" a mortgage**, which refers to a seller retaining the mortgage and the liability for payments, but the new owner would pay the mortgage payments
- **liquidated damages**, which refers to a clause specifying particular amounts due to an aggrieved party, such as a seller keeping the deposit/earnest money in the event of breach
- **settlement or closing instructions**, which details who pays for what, such as tax prorations, property repairs, title insurance, and other transaction expenses

A contract **contingency** is a **special condition** or provision inserted by either party that must be met in order for an approved offer to become a fully binding contract. **In the event the contingency is not satisfied, the contract is considered void**. *(In practice, disputes may arise.)*

Common contingencies include
- **financing**, which typically asserts that the contract is contingent on the buyer's being approved for a certain type of loan by a particular date
- **property sale**, which typically asserts that a buyer's current property must be sold prior to the target closing date for the new property
- **structural survey**, which typically asserts that a **professional home inspection report** must show that the true condition of the property is acceptable to the buyer

Once all of the contract details have been negotiated and there is a binding contract, each party acquires certain **contractual rights and responsibilities**. Some of these include

- **equitable title**, which means that the buyer, during the executory period of contract fulfillment, has a property interest, specifically **the right to acquire formal legal title**, which in turn **may allow the buyer to transfer or assign that right**
- **assignment**, which means that the buyer may transfer their rights in a property
- **rescission**, which means that one of the parties, generally through a contract-specific contingency or during a regulated-sale review period, may **rescind**, or cancel the contract without penalty – this term refers to "unmaking" a contract and **restoring the parties to their precontractual position, including the return of all monies**

A variety of events can **terminate offers and counteroffers**, many of which are examples of conditions that arise **by operation of law**, which means that existing laws make them happen automatically, without any direct action or intent of a party. Some of the events that may terminate an offer or counteroffer include the

- **death or incapacity** of a party to the proposed contract, which automatically voids an offer or counteroffer, since there has been **no completed offer and acceptance**
- **bankruptcy** of one of the parties
- **expiration** of a contractual time period

Several events may **terminate a sales contract**, most obviously the **completion** of the sale and transfer of title at closing/settlement. As noted previously, this means that all contractual commitments have been **fully performed**, or **discharged**. Sales contracts may also be terminated by such occurrences as

- **failure to satisfy a contract contingency**
- **eminent domain/compulsory purchase** proceedings

However, in the case of any contract termination, **one or both parties may incur liabilities** that may be remedied by either existing contractual agreements or litigation.

Breach of contract means a legally unsupportable violation of any of the contract terms by either party and generally gives rise to legal disputes over how to either pursue or abandon the contract. In the event that **contract disputes** arise during the executory period, legal action may follow.

Common **remedies for a breach** include seeking

- **contract rescission**, which basically means cancellation and return of deposits
- **specific performance**, which is a **judicial remedy** that requires getting a court order for the party who breached the contract to honor it
- **monetary damages**, which is another **judicial remedy** that means getting a court-ordered payment of financial restitution
- **liquidated damages**, which is a **nonjudicial remedy** that means getting whatever any **liquidated damages provision** in the contract stipulates, **such as the forfeiture of earnest money** in the case of buyer default

Leases: Types and Elements of Leasehold Estates, Leases, Lease Clauses

As noted in Topic Area I-A, *estates in real property* are divided into *freehold* and *leasehold estates*.

> *Although the various names of leasehold estate typically use the terms "**estate**" and "**tenancy**" interchangeably; the convention here, as in both common practice and on most test questions, will be to use "tenancy."*

Leasehold estates are contracts, and **are classified as personal property**, **not real property**. Therefore, whereas they typically entitle the lessee to all of the possession-and-use rights of ownership, **they do not entitle the lessee to transfer title, encumber it with liens, or make alterations to the property** without the knowledge and consent of the owner *(i.e., multi-unit developers such as Manor House or Inwood)*.

Types of leasehold estates include

- **tenancy for years**, which means that there is **a definite termination date**. **Vacation rentals** as well as **commercial leases** are often written this way, and may run for whatever time period suits both parties, such as June 1 through August 31 for the former, or a few days for storage to many years for an industrial site for the latter.

- **tenancy from period to period**, or **periodic tenancy**, which means there is **no definite termination date, just recurring time periods** during which one party or the other may exercise an option to terminate it. This is a **common tenancy arrangement in residential leases, which may start as a tenancy for years**, generally one, and then, through an automatic renewal, or 'evergreen' clause, renew for the same period and general terms.

- **tenancy at will**, which is **similar to a tenancy from period to period except that there is no specified periodic nature** to it – it is simply at the will and discretion of the landlord and may be terminated at almost any time by either party. These situations may include an owner letting a tenant remain in a property being taken by eminent domain right up to the last minute, or tenants being given the option to move out whenever a job transfer or alternate housing situation arises.

- **tenancy at sufferance**, which means that a tenant has **refused to vacate** at the end of a tenancy for years or periodic tenancy and **remains in possession of the property against the will of the landlord**. Generally, a landlord will not accept or cash rent checks to avoid appearing to approve the tenant's continuation.
    - **tenant at sufferance**, or **holdover tenant**, are terms used to describe a tenant who remains against the landlord's will in a tenancy at sufferance
        - *the term **holdover tenant** may also be used to identify any tenant who extends an initial lease period, whether it is at sufferance or by renewal – read questions with this term carefully to be sure which one is intended*

The names of various common lease types suggest the financial structure of the revenues, or *method of payment*. Some of these include

- **gross lease**, which means the **tenant pays a flat fee out of which the landlord pays all standard property expenses**, such as taxes, association fees, and, in some cases, utilities. **Most residential leases are gross leases**.

- *net lease*, under which the **tenant pays a base rent and some or all of the property expenses**, beginning with utilities, taxes, and special assessments
- *full-service lease* is a lease in which **the landlord agrees to pay all maintenance, property taxes, and insurance**
- *percentage leases* have a **fixed base rental fee plus a percentage of the gross or net income in excess of a predetermined minimum sales volume**; these are **common in retail properties**
- *graduated leases*, which establish a **schedule for rent increases, generally based on a business tenant's anticipated growth** of gross or net income
- *index leases* are **similar to graduated leases, but the rental amounts may go up or down, generally in reference to the consumer price index (CPI)** or the cost-of-living index
- *lease purchase*, which is **typically a rent-to-own arrangement** where an agreed-upon portion of the rent is applied toward the purchase price and either when the tenant can arrange other financing or when the full price is paid, ownership transfers; *not commonly done in Bermuda*
- *lease-option*, or *lease with an option to buy*, is a mixture of a lease and a purchase contract, but begins as **a lease with a clause allowing the tenant to exercise an option to purchase the property**

Some other types of leases refer to the **property type** rather than payment type. Examples of these include

- *ground lease*, or *land lease*, generally is **a long-term commercial or industrial lease of land only, with the tenant typically erecting a building** that reverts to the landowner at the end of the rental period, which may be as long as 99 years. **Ground leases are commonly structured and paid as some form of net lease**.

Leases may include any or all of the following **common provisions or clauses**

- *covenant of quiet enjoyment*, which entitles the tenant to **undisturbed possession and use of the property**. Most leases qualify this right to allow the landlord to enter the premises periodically during business hours for maintenance and inspections, as well as for emergencies.
- *term of lease provision*, which generally **gives the start and end dates, may also, in the case of a periodic residential lease, include an automatic renewal provision**, or *evergreen clause*, which extends the lease unless one of the parties specifically terminates it according to the process indicated in the provision
- *escalator clause*, or *escalation clause*, or *step-up clause*, which **specifies the terms and conditions of rent increases**; they are central to graduated leases, though they can be found in any lease and are commonly incorporated into multi-year office-space leases
- *right of first refusal* clause may be included in a lease when the tenant wants the opportunity to purchase the property in the event the owner decides to sell; **it gives the tenant the right to review any sales offer the owner receives and either match it or else let the owner proceed with a sale to a different party**
- *subletting*, or *subleasing*, which refers to a **tenant leasing the property to someone else**. When not prohibited, **the original tenant remains primarily liable to the landlord for rents and property condition**.

- *assignment* refers to a tenant *transferring the lease and some or all of its liability to a another person*. In some cases, the landlord or the lease will allow the complete substitution of the original tenant by the new tenant regarding lease responsibilities and let the new tenant assume sole, primary responsibility for the rest of the lease period.

Options

As noted above, an *option* can refer to completely different situations, but typically an *option is a type of unilateral contract*, which is *binding on the seller to sell, but not on the buyer to buy*.

There are two primary applications of the term option. They are

- *an option*, which is most often in a *commercial property purchase offer* and serves to hold a property open for a specified period at a specified price *in exchange for some monetary consideration*, which is *generally (1) applied toward the purchase price* if all of the conditions are met and the sale goes through, *or (2) kept by the owner if there is no sale*, and
- *a lease-option*, or *lease with an option to buy*, which is a mixture of a lease and a purchase contract, that begins as *a lease with a clause allowing the tenant to exercise an option to purchase the property*.

I-E. Financing, Types of Loans, and Loan Provisions

Financing Sources

Financing sources for buyers who either cannot or simply prefer not to pay cash include *lending institutions*, *the seller*, and, of course, family, friends, and personal contacts.

In most cases, though, buyers will make arrangements with *a local bank* for property financing. *The local bank or financial institution that originates the loan* represents what is known as the *primary mortgage market*, or *primary market*.

In turn, the local bank will simultaneously be making loans to other buyers, and eventually have a collection, or *portfolio*, of loans. These loans, as a group, may look attractive to a larger financial institution as a *secured investment*. Once a loan is sold as part of a package like this, it has entered into what is known as the *secondary mortgage market*, or *secondary market*.

If the bank sells its portfolio of loans to a financial investor, the bank regains its capital while shifting the ownership, and risk of default, to the institution in the secondary market. The local bank now has the funds available to make new loans, create a new portfolio, and sell it off. And so the cycle goes.

Sale and leaseback, *sale/leaseback*, or simply *leaseback* is an arrangement by which a property owner, usually commercial, sells the property to an investor with the understanding that the seller may lease the property from the buyer immediately. This arrangement is often *made to free up capital for use by the former owner*, now the lessee.

Seller-financing is another source of funding for a buyer, and property-secured income for the seller. Some of the particulars of seller-financing will be presented below, and were noted above under *contract for deed (land contract)*.

Types of Loans

Types of loans include a host of ordinary, special, and creative financing options in lending. For the sake of broad categorizations here, loan types can be separated by three primary elements: *loan purpose*, *repayment options*, and *interest rates*. Clearly, all three categories are present in every loan.

Note: The term *"mortgage"* may be substituted for *"loan"* as soon as it is clear that *the loan is, or will be, secured by real property*. *However, "loan" is used here as the default term to keep the primary focus on the basic financing arrangements*. *The test questions may use the terms interchangeably as appropriate to the topic being tested.*

- Types of loans with names that suggest their *loan purpose or primary characteristic* include
  - *construction loans*, or *interim loans*, or *drawdown*, are loans that are generally paid to the borrower in installments during the course of a construction project. They typically require the borrower to make interest-only payments and arrange for *permanent financing* of some sort at the end of the construction period.
  - *blanket loans* 'cover' more than one lot, parcel, or property; they are common in subdivision developments, and typically include a *partial release clause*, which allows the borrower to *pay off and release separate parcels* as they get sold
  - *package loans* include funding to purchase *personal as well as real property*, as in the sale of a furnished condo
  - *wraparound loans* allow a borrower to take out *a second loan*, make a payment *large enough to cover both loans* to the new lender, and have *the new lender make the payments on the original loan*
  - *open-end loans* offer a line of credit secured by a property, and are usually created for improvements that will be done in stages, so the borrower's monthly indebtedness keeps pace with actual outlays
  - *home equity* loans are typically made on an agreed amount of a homeowner's equity in the property, either in a lump sum or a line of credit. They are often referred to as *second mortgages*, or *junior mortgages*, and typically have a lien priority below any other existing mortgages.
  - *reverse annuity mortgages* provide payments from a bank to the homeowner, who generally has already paid off any original loans. This is an increasingly popular form of financing among retirement-aged homeowners who want to have access to their equity and leave repayment to their estate or heirs.
  - *bridge loans*, or *swing loans*, both often referred to as *gap financing*, are short-term loans made to cover a temporary shortfall or period prior to the funding of the permanent loan

- *nonrecourse loans* are secured loans that allow the lender to attach only the collateral, leaving all other borrower assets judgment-proof in the event of borrower default

- Types of loans with names that suggest their *repayment options* include
  - *amortized loans* are those that are paid off over time, usually through equal monthly payments for a set number of years
    - *fully amortized loans*, or *level-payment loans*, are structured to pay down the loan amount, plus interest, in *equal payments*, generally paid monthly until the balance is zero. These loans begin with a higher portion of each installment going toward the interest, and end with most of the loan payment being applied directly to the remaining principal.
    - *partially amortized loans* can be structured any number of ways, but typically mean that the loan amount is paid down according to an agreed-upon schedule, with a final payment that is larger than the others
      - *balloon payment* is the term applied to this sort of large final payment
  - *growing equity mortgages* have payments that increase over time with the additional amount applied directly to principal, which brings down the interest payments and overall repayment period of the loan
  - *graduated payment loans* are fixed-rate, scheduled payment loans that allow the borrower to make lower payments initially, and increase them to make up for the difference. Similar to growing equity mortgages, they both are structured in anticipation of the borrower's income rising along with the payments due.
  - *term loans*, or *straight loans*, or *straight note*, look similar to a partially amortized loan in that they have single, level payments for the life of the loan with a much larger final payment. However, under a term loan, the *payments are interest-only*, and *the entire principal amount is due* at the end of the loan's *term*, or time period for the borrower to use the capital.

- Types of loans with names that identify their *interest rate structure* include
  - *fixed-rate loans*, which have an interest rate that remains the same for the life of the loan
  - *adjustable-rate mortgages (ARMs)*, which have a fluctuating interest rate that gets adjusted at periodic intervals. They typically allow a borrower to pay a lower rate for the first few years, which keeps their initial expenses low, then adjusts either to a preset interest rate or a rate based on market conditions at an adjustment interval.

Seller financing may take the form of a *purchase-money mortgage*, or seller *carryback*, in which the seller generally provides *a supplementary loan* to the buyer that makes up the difference between the purchase price and the total of the buyer's other loans and cash.

Or, it may take the form of primary financing under a *contract for deed (land contract)*.

Seller financing is attractive in situations where lenders are reluctant to lend, such as raw land, or when the seller wants to either spread out the receipt of proceeds or 'play bank' and collect the interest.

A seller may also elect this option simply to help close the gap on a sale where the buyer's other financing and available cash fall short of the purchase price.

The *terms of repayment* and the *creation of a security instrument* may be structured in a variety of ways for both *purchase-money mortgages* and a *contract for deed (land contract)*, depending on negotiations between the seller and the buyer.

Loan Provisions

Some of the more common clauses in a financing agreement include
- *acceleration clause,* which allows the lender to call the entire remaining debt due on default, or after a certain number of consecutive late payments
- *alienation clause*, also known as a *due-on-sale clause*, which allows the lender to call the entire balance of the loan due-and-payable upon the transfer of the property
- *defeasance clause*, which requires the lender to provide a *release of mortgage*, or *satisfaction of mortgage*, document when the loan has been repaid; this document can be recorded in the public record to assert that the lien has been removed.
  > *In the case of financing by a deed of trust, this document is known as a **release deed**, or **deed of reconveyance**.*
- *subordination clause*, which serves to clarify that a loan will accept *a subordinate*, or *junior*, *position* and remain *behind another loan in the priority order of liens*. It is a common clause in second mortgages, although some commercial lenders require borrowers to get existing loan holders to allow their loans to be made secondary to the new loan through a *subordination agreement*.
  - *subrogation, an insurance term regarding an insurance company's right to pay a claim and then collect directly from the responsible party, may appear as a similar-looking-word type of distractor for subordination*
- *prepayment clause*, or *prepayment penalty clause*, helps lenders increase their return when a borrower pays off a loan ahead of schedule by charging a fee for early payoffs. *Once quite common*, they are now often subject to regulatory limits, and *they are prohibited in some loans*.

Other clauses and provisions that arise in lending, and may appear as distractors, include
- *partial release clause*, or *release clause*, as noted above under blanket mortgages, allow a borrower who has a single loan covering several properties to sell one, pay off its share to the lender, and receive a release of its property description in the lien from the lender
- *escalator clause* may be included in a loan document to *allow the lender to increase the interest rate in the event the borrower makes late payments* or is in default
  - *an escalator clause, or escalation clause, may also refer to a clause in leases that allows rent changes based on inflation or changing market conditions, such as taxes or operating expenses – if this term appears in a test question, it will be clear whether it applies to a loan or a lease*

- *assumption clause* may be included in a loan document to *either prohibit or allow a borrower to pass along the loan obligation to a subsequent buyer*. In some cases, the original borrower remains liable for the loan in the event the new owner defaults. But *a lender may release the original borrower through* the process of
  - *novation*, which means *substituting one party to a contract for another*, thus releasing the first party from further obligation while shifting that obligation to the new party alone
- *nondisturbance clause* may be in a mortgage for properties that are rented, and states that the lender will not terminate leases in the event of foreclosure
  - *assignment of rents* may also be included in mortgages on rental properties, and gives the lender the right to collect rents directly in the event of borrower default

Pertinent Financing Concepts and Terminology

Financing instruments can be intricately tailored to the particular situation, and involve a lot of time-honored as well as new and creative concepts.

Some of the more common terms in property financing include
- *equity*, which refers to *the amount of principal a property owner has in the property*. For example, if an owner has a $250,000 mortgage on a property worth $850,000, the owner's equity in the property is $600,000.
- *loan-to-value ratio (LTV, or L/V)* is a ratio *obtained by dividing the loan amount by the property value*, which is taken from the lesser of the appraised value or the sales price. For example, a loan of $80,000 on a property valued at $100,000 has an LTV of 80 percent. Clearly, *the lower the LTV, the lower the risk of loss for the lender* in the event a borrower defaults and the lender has to sell the property.
- *leverage*, which refers to *the amount of money borrowed in relation to the property's value* – *high leverage* equates to a *low down payment* and *a large loan amount*, or a *high LTV*
- *buy-downs* refer to an *up-front sum paid by a borrower specifically to reduce the interest rate and thereby bring down the monthly payment*. The reduced rate may be temporary or permanent, depending on the arrangement.
- *annual percentage rate (APR)* is the term for the *effective* annual percentage rate, or *true annual cost of borrowing*; it allows more accurate consumer comparisons of lenders and financing offers by taking into account all loan charges and fees, such as points and prepaid interest, rather than just identifying the interest rate applied to the loan balance. *In the United States, APR details are defined and regulated by the* **Truth in Lending Act, Regulation Z***.*
- *usury* refers to *a lender's charging an illegally high rate of interest*. *Usury laws vary* among jurisdictions and do not even apply in some.
  - *The term originally applied to charging* **any** *interest on loans and is still* **commonly defined as charging exorbitantly high interest***; in legal terms it refers to charging a rate in excess of legal limits.* **Though Bermuda lacks a specific usury law, this financially relevant concept is still valid for testing***.*

- *yield* is the term for the *return* or *profit* a lender makes on a transaction, *generally expressed as a percentage of the amount invested*
- *points* refer to a measurement unit for loan costs -- *one point* equals *one percent of the face value of the loan*

Lender requirements and obligations

Lender requirements and obligations include those they make of borrowers as well as those expected of them by borrowers and the law.

The process of reviewing an applicant for a loan typically includes the following components and considerations
- *prequalification* generally refers to a lender, or even a licensee, determining the probable maximum loan amount the borrower can support by collecting preliminary information about the borrower's financial circumstances, generally during a brief interview. It is a nonbinding preliminary assessment.
- *qualification* refers to the process a lender goes through of more closely reviewing a buyer's credit and financial status to determine the actual maximum loan amount the lender would fund. Once approved for funding, the applicant becomes known as a *qualified buyer*, or *approved buyer*.
    > *The terms **prequalified**, or **preapproved**, are sometimes applied to a fully qualified buyer who is looking for property, as in, "My client has been prequalified by a lender for the amount of financing given in this offer."*
- *credit report* from a major credit reporting agency will be requested by the lender to determine the official status of an applicant's financial history

When a prospective buyer, qualified or not, finds a property and approaches the lender for funding, the lender will perform a property review prior to fully approving the loan. The process of reviewing a property for a loan typically includes the following components and considerations
- *property appraisal* for a current estimate of value
- *title search* or *attorney's opinion of title*, to confirm that the title is unencumbered
- *property survey*, if there are any questions about the exact boundaries and possible encroachments or physical encumbrances
- *zoning codes and ordinances* that govern the use and future of the property

Lenders may also require some of the following additional charges and conditions as part of the processing and funding of certain loans
- *discount points*, often simply called *points*, are *a lender's up-front charge* for making a loan; *points are typically charged to increase the lender's yield when funding a loan at below-market interest rates*; as noted above, one point equals one percent of the loan amount
- *bank finder's fee,* which is a lender's *charge for preparing and processing a loan*
- *document preparation*, or *"doc prep,"* which is a lender's *charge for preparing and copying loan-related documents*
- *funding fee*, which is another type of lender's processing charge

I. Principles and Practices of Real Estate (40 questions)

I-F. Mortgages, Deeds, and Title Issues

Financing Instruments: Mortgages, Contracts for Deed, Deeds of Trust

An *instrument* is a written legal document or contract defining rights, duties, and other obligations; a *secured instrument* is one that has a some form of *collateral* identified as *alternate compensation* in the event the borrower *defaults*, or fails to perform, according to the instrument, or contract.

Secured instruments for real estate property loans are broadly termed *mortgages*.

A mortgage typically has a *note*, or *promissory note*, which is *the financing instrument* that serves as *evidence of the debt* and *details the terms of repayment*, and the *mortgage*, which is *the security instrument that creates a lien* on the property *as security for the loan*.

A common way of expressing this is that a *borrower secures the note by signing the mortgage*.

Two key terms for mortgage instruments are
- *hypothecate*, which is *to pledge property as security* for a debt *while retaining possession, title, and use of the property*
- *pledge*, which is *to provide something as security* for a debt, *generally by surrendering possession but not full title*; commonly illustrated by a pawn shop's holding of personal property as collateral in exchange for a short-term loan

Three of the more common ways of structuring mortgages include
- the ordinary *mortgage*, which is a *two-party instrument* between a borrower and an institutional lender. Typically, the borrower, or *mortgagor*, pledges the property as security against default and retains the title, and the lender, or *mortgagee*, gives the agreed-upon financing for the borrower to acquire the property in exchange for the legal right to force the sale of the property in the event of default.
- a *deed of trust*, or *trust deed*, which is a *three-party instrument* under which a borrower, known as the *trustor*, and an institutional lender, known as the *beneficiary*, have a third party, known as the *trustee*, hold the property's legal title "in trust" until the debt is repaid.
  - *in the event of default, lender foreclosure rights are generally more direct under a deed of trust financing arrangement than under a two-party mortgage*

Deeds and Warranties

As noted above, a *deed* is *a written instrument by which land is conveyed*. There are several areas of note about deeds: terminology, elements of validity, common types of deeds, covenants and warranties, and title issues.

The *terminology* for parties to a deed includes knowing that the one who is *granting*, or giving away, ownership is referred to as the *grantor*, and the new owner is known as the *grantee*.

There are some *legal elements of validity* that are required in order for a deed to be legally *valid* and *enforceable*. While some states require a few more than others, most require, at a minimum, the following elements or conditions

- it must be *in writing*
- the grantor must have *legal capacity*, that is, be of legal age and mental competence
- *identification of the parties*, that is, the grantor and the grantee must be named
- *statement of consideration*, or what is being paid/exchanged for the property. Often expressed as a nominal sum, as in "for $10 and other good and valuable consideration"; many contemporary transfers specify the actual sales price
- *words of conveyance*, or a *granting clause*, such as, "I do hereby grant and convey"
- *a legal description of the property*
- *signature of the grantor*
- *delivery* and *acceptance*

In some jurisdictions, there are additional requirements, such as

- an *habendum clause*, which defines the extent and limitations of the interest conveyed; it generally begins with the words "to have and to hold," and so is often referred to as the *"to-have-and-to-hold" clause*. Sometimes it is considered part of the granting clause.
- a *seal*, or mark of authentication. It is often just the printed, or written, word "Seal" by the line for the grantor's signature.

Other common parts and processes of deed creation may include

- the *date*
- *relevant exceptions and restrictions*
- *acknowledgement*, or formal statement that the grantee is the one signing the deed and is doing so voluntarily
- *recording* the deed in the public records to provide notice of its existence

  Recording the deed provides *constructive notice that the title has been transferred* to the new owner.

  This is critically important in protecting an owner's title interest, since *proper, legal recording establishes a new owner's position and rights within the chain of title*.

  The specific process for recording deeds and other documents *may* involve formal *acknowledgments* of signatures by witnesses and/or *notarization* in order to create a legally valid recordation; *the process details for recording documents are jurisdiction-specific.*

Types of deeds are as varied as the purposes they serve and the *covenants and warranties* they include. Some of the more common types of deeds are

- *general warranty deeds*, or *warranty deeds*, which *include all of the five covenants listed below*, and *offer the greatest protection for the grantee of all deeds*

- *special warranty deeds*, which warrant the *title against title defects that arose <u>only </u>during the grantor's ownership*
- *bargain and sale deeds*, which contain **no guaranty from the grantor about the validity of title, but implies that the grantor has an interest** that is being sold to the grantee
- *quitclaim deeds*, which have **no covenants or warranties**. They simply relinquish any and all interest the grantor may have in a property. They are commonly used to ensure that a particular party will not decide to interfere later; ***they provide the least protection for the grantee*** against other potential problems with the title.

The following ***additional types of deeds*** are less common than those above but do appear in various national textbooks. ***Some are jurisdiction-specific or go by different names in different jurisdictions, so are not fair game for testing, except as distractors.*** They include

- *mortgage deeds, which are deeds whereby a property owner borrowing money secured by the property gives a lender, who is sometimes the seller using this deed for seller-financing,* **legal title and contractual rights** *to claim and/or sell the property if the borrower is in breach of loan provisions;* **this is an increasingly popular financing instrument for the sale and resale of European timeshares**.
- *gift deeds, which are deeds given for either a nominal sum or "love and affection"*
- *executor's deeds, or* **administrator's deeds**, *which are used in some jurisdictions to convey property from the estate of a deceased owner*

Special note*: since* **trust deeds**, *or* **deeds of trust**, *are* **mortgage financing instruments**, *the term(s) would only appear in this Topic Area as a distractor.*

Deeds generally include a variety of ***covenants and warranties***. Covenants are ***formal agreements or promises***; warranties are ***guarantees***. The ***five most common*** are the

- *covenant of seisin*, which means the grantor claims to be the owner of the property and is therefore legally entitled to convey it
- *covenant of quiet enjoyment*, which means the grantor promises that no one will disturb the new owner with claims against the property, such as an undisclosed co-owner or a long-lost heir; *since this term is also used as a lease provision, wherever it appears on the exam, the question will clarify whether it refers to leases or deeds*
- *covenant of further assurance*, which means the grantor assumes responsibility for any additional documentation necessary to ensure the grantee's title, such as releases from family members who should have signed the original transfer deed
- *covenant against encumbrances*, which means the grantor promises that any and all easements or liens have been properly disclosed and is liable for damages if others are discovered after the transfer
- *covenant of warranty forever*, or *warranty of title*, which means the grantor promises to bear the cost of defending the title against undiscovered or undisclosed flaws existing at the time of transfer – sometimes seen as synonymous with the covenant of quiet enjoyment

Title Issues

Regardless of which type of deed is used to convey and/or warrant title, there may be a ***defect in the title***, or something that might put a ***cloud on the title***, meaning that there are conflicting claims that prevent the absolute legal conveyance of ***clear title***.

> ***Common defects*** include ***forged documents*** or ***undisclosed third-party interests***, such as liens, ***undiscovered ownership interests*** of spouses or family members, ***unrecorded prior transfers or assignments***, or a ***lis pendens***, which is Latin for ***"a pending law suit."***

A professional ***title search*** generally discovers all of the recorded information about the property's ***liens***, ***lis pendens***, and ***chain of title***.

> *This chain may extend from the present back to the original owner, who may have received title through a **grant** from the King of England or, in some American states, another foreign ruler. However, local convention in many jurisdictions only requires searching the past 40-60 years; **in Bermuda it is 20 years – see Topic Area VI-B, The Conveyancing Act 1983**.*

> *In some jurisdictions, attorneys handle basic title searches and then prepare an **attorney's opinion of title,** whereas in others the name for the most thorough type of search, which summarizes all documents in all official sources, is an **abstract of title**, and is performed by an **abstractor**.*

If the search identifies a ***cloud on the title***, it may be resolved through a ***quiet title action*** or ***quiet title suit***, or ***suit to quiet title***, which is a court pleading that leads to a judge's decision on the matter. Or the cloud may also be lifted, and the need for a quiet title action removed, by ***getting a quitclaim deed*** from the newly discovered party with a real, or potential, interest in the property.

I-G. Settlement/Closing

Procedures

Note*: according to legal sources, "'settlement' and 'closing' can be and are used interchangeably."* *So, despite local preferences and conventions that favor the use of one over the other, in most cases here and on examinations, "settlement" will be used.*

Note the following terms for both professional exposure and testing purposes
- ***conveyance attorney*** or ***purchaser attorney*** are common terms for the ***settlement agent*** authorised to process the settlement details
- ***escrow*** is a generic legal term used to refer to each of the following descriptions
    - ***an account,*** as in, "We put the money in escrow." In this sense, escrow is interchangeable with ***escrow account*** or ***trust account***

> • *the 'signed-contract to delivered-deed' period* of a real estate transaction, as in, "The property is in escrow."

Style Note: To avoid confusion, test questions generally refer to a property sales transaction account as an **escrow/trust account**, thereby providing the respective key word that allows all candidates to readily understand, within the context of question, that it is about a sales transaction situation rather than an office trust account.

The settlement agent acts in a fiduciary, or highly trusted, capacity regarding all transaction funds and details.

As a fiduciary, the settlement agent has an obligation of accounting, which means the agent is obligated to avoid either of the following situations with transaction-related funds

- • *commingling*, which means mingling, or combining, transaction funds with other funds that are required to be maintained separately. This could result from putting the funds in the wrong account, either business or personal.
- • *conversion*, which refers to converting funds to another use than intended, or misappropriating them, as in using earnest money to pay office expenses. Conversion is generally preceded by commingling.

Further, the settlement agent oversees the checklist of details and contingencies created by the purchase/sales contract and loans. These may include such elements as

- • securing the **satisfaction and release of contingencies**
- • verifying the documentation necessary for the **satisfaction and release of liens**
- • gathering and reviewing documents regarding **encumbrances**, **restrictions**, **title and property insurance**, and other contract-specific requirements
- • **disbursing transaction funds** according to **priority of liens**, which generally get paid, first to last, in the following order
    - • *property taxes*
    - • *special assessments*
    - • *first mortgage*
    - • *other liens*, generally by date of recordation
    - • *other settlement/closing fees*
    - • *balance*, if any, *to the seller*, or foreclosed owner
- • *proper distribution* of pertinent documents, e.g., releases for any extinguished lien(s) and/or encumbrance(s); new deed and lien(s)

Closing Costs

Some questions in this area focus on which party is responsible for certain charges, but this section has a heavy representation of math questions.

Many of the costs involved in a real estate transfer *are negotiable*, even when convention has one party or the other as typically responsible. Common costs and responsible parties include

- *buyer's closing costs*, where applicable
  - *refunds to seller* of prorated portion of remaining rent, taxes, insurance, condo fees, other prepaid utility and property expenses
  - *deed and new mortgage fees*
  - *appraisal fees for loan funding*
  - *building survey/home inspection fees*
  - *new loan fees*
- *seller's closing costs*, where applicable
  - *cost of clearing title*
  - *loan payoff*
  - *agent's commission*

MATH Questions!!

Real estate finance, especially settlement, provides another area for math questions, but probably no more than *between two and four math* questions will be based on topics found in this Topic Area. The questions will provide all the numbers and information necessary to do the math.

The topics are most likely to concentrate on areas that a licensee *might reasonably need to compute to confirm or correct figures provided on a settlement statement*. These would include, but not be limited to, the following situations

- *principal, interest, tax, and insurance (PITI)* totals and sub-parts for impound accounts
- *property taxes*, prorations and determination from assessed value and mill rate
- *property insurance premiums* and prorated portions
- *prorations of prepaid expenses*, including municipal sewer and water charges, unused heating oil or propane amounts, other property maintenance or association fees. *Note – these may be prorated and credited/debited to either party depending on when recurring fees are due and/or were paid*
- *mortgages – interest payments* and *principal balance* at particular times
- *prorations of rents* at closing
- *special assessment charges*
- *agent's commission*
- *property sales price determinations* from a variable, such as taxes due, commission paid, or a LTV percentage and loan amount
- *buyer's total cost of purchase*
- *seller's net after sale*

In most cases, *all* conditions of who pays for what will be included in the math questions, as will any clarification about whether prorations are based on a 360-day year with 30-day months or a 365-day calendar year.

As previously noted, most of the math questions on the test are not particularly complicated. Those that are simply require you to take a deep breath and think a little harder. Chances are that you will be able to at least rule out a few of the answer choices and then be able to make a better-odds guess at whatever's left.

For those of you with math anxiety, one strategy for tackling them is to mark them on your answer sheet as soon as they appear, then move on immediately to the next question. After answering all of the <u>non-math</u> questions, you can then return to <u>JUST</u> the math questions and work them as a group, doing the ones that look easiest first.

Documents

Settlement documents required will vary according to the specifics of the transaction. Also, the **information covered in previous areas may lend some questions to this area if the thrust is more on the document than the process**.

However, common documents in the sale of a residential property secured by a loan include
- *deed* for the real property included in the transaction
- *bill(s) of sale* for all personal (unattached) property included in the transaction
- *property insurance* as required
- *reduction certificate*, which is a loan document that shows the remaining principal balance, interest rate, and date of maturity; it is used to verify the terms and amount of an existing loan that a buyer will be assuming as well as by a seller who needs to know the exact payoff amount on the day of closing
- *satisfaction piece*, or *satisfaction of mortgage*, which is the certificate a mortgagee provides to a mortgagor that states the debt has been paid; typically it is recorded to confirm the title is free of the lien encumbrance

I-H. Property Management and Investments

Property Management Considerations

A *property management contract* defines the relationship between a property manager and an owner. Through the contract, the owner typically authorizes the *property manager to act as a general agent*, able to make a wide range of binding decisions in the course of managing the property. These activities include, but are not limited to, the authority to
- *select tenants*
- *prepare and sign leases*
- *collect and deposit rents*
- *hire and pay employees*
- *contract* with maintenance and repair contractors
- *make risk management decisions*, such as selecting insurance coverages

- *prepare operating budgets*
- *determine gross effective income*
- *maintain office accounts*
- *monitor and pay fixed operating expenses* such as salaries and taxes
- *establish a reserve account* for variable expenses, such as repairs and supplies

The property management agreement itself generally includes the following *key elements*
- *property description*
- *contract period and termination provisions*
- *property management's duties, scope of authority, and limitations*
- *statement of the owner's purpose or objective*, such as maximizing income or increasing property value
    - *trying to achieve the owner's objective is generally considered to be the primary duty of a property manager*
- *statement of the owner's obligations and duties*
- *frequency and types of reporting to the owner*
- *management compensation arrangements*, which are generally based on a percentage of gross rental income. However rates for property management services *are established by negotiation between the principal and the property manager*

Fixtures, mentioned in Topic Area I-A, are of special importance in leased property. Generally, anything a residential tenant attaches to a rental unit in a permanent manner can be argued as becoming real property and thus must be left in the unit at the end of the lease term.

Trade fixtures are more commonly understood to remain the tenant's property, though all tenant-provided *improvements*, both residential and commercial, should be spelled out to avoid confusion.

The transfer of ownership of improvements is known as *accession*, and is often part of an owner's *reversionary right*, which refers to *the reinstatement of the owner's full ownership and possession rights at the end of the lease period.*

The *sale or other transfer of rental property* ownership during a lease period *typically has no effect on existing leases* – new owners must honor the terms of all leases. *Exceptions* include *some foreclosure sales* and *most eminent domain/compulsory purchase actions*.

Abandonment refers to a tenant's *vacating a rental property prior to the end of the lease term and defaulting on the rent*. A term related to the property of a tenant in default is
- *distrain*, or *distress*, which refers to the right of a landlord, generally after a court order, to seize a tenant's personal property for rent in arrears *(see Topic Area VI-G, Landlord and Tenant Act 1974 for more Bermuda-specific laws on this subject)*.

Evictions may be *initiated by either the landlord or the tenant*. Although they are handled according to jurisdiction-specific processes, they are commonly referred to by the same terms

- *actual eviction* is the *landlord's recourse* when a tenant has breached the lease, such as nonpayment of rent or exceeding the occupancy limit. This is typically effected by the landlord's bringing a *suit for possession* in court; *the legal details and timing vary from place to place.*
- *constructive eviction* is the *tenant's recourse* when the landlord has breached the lease by *letting the property become uninhabitable through conscious neglect*. This kind of neglect on the part of the landlord *relieves the tenant from the obligation to pay rent*. *Again, though, the details of the process may vary from place to place*.

In the course of renting properties, *the landlord or owner has to pay attention to many of the same fair housing, lending, and credit laws that govern property sales*, plus some handicapped access requirements and property condition disclosures.

These will be covered in specific detail in the appropriate following Topic Areas, most notably in VI-G, The Landlord and Tenant Act 1974 and VI-H, The Human Rights Act 1981. However, it is worth summarizing the broad obligations of the latter in this Topic Area

- *The Human Rights Act 1981* includes the body of subsequent amendments and applies to rental housing as well as housing sales.
  - This Act provides *protection against discrimination in the sale, <u>rental</u>, or <u>advertising</u> of residential property* for the following *protected classes* based on the following personal characteristics (*see Topic Area VI-H for more*)
    - *race*
    - *place of origin, <u>including Bermuda</u>*
    - *colour*
    - *ethnic or national origins*
    - *sex or sexual orientation*
    - *marital status*
    - *disability*
    - *family status, including but not restricted to*
      - *condition of having been born out of lawful wedlock*
      - *current pregnancy regardless of marital status*
    - *religion or beliefs*
    - *political opinions*
    - *criminal record, except where there are valid reasons relevant to the nature of the particular offence for which he is convicted that would justify the difference in treatment*

Investments

One approach to valuation, the *income approach*, is primarily applicable to investment properties, so information from I-C is duplicated here, where it has the most direct application.

The *income approach*, estimates the present value of future net income of income-producing properties through the process of *capitalization*, which converts *future income projections into current value*.

> The *income approach is generally the most applicable when analyzing investment properties*, such as retail, commercial, industrial, and residential rental properties.

Using *the income approach*, a licensee would estimate the present value of future net income of income-producing properties through the process of *capitalization*, which converts *future income projections into current value*.

> The *income approach* is *based on the principle of anticipation*, which asserts that value is created by the expectation of benefits to be derived from *return on investment* during ownership as well as any capital gain realized at resale.

> The *capitalization rate*, or *cap rate*, is the term for the *rate of return* on the cost of the investment.

> To *compute the capitalization rate* for a particular property, simply *divide the property's net operating income (NOI) by its price*.
> - For example, a $2,000,000 property that has a $200,000/year NOI has a capitalization rate of 10 percent.

> The following *three categories of income* are important to remember for rentals and other investment properties. *The third is the one to use for computing cap rates.*
>   - *potential gross income*, or *projected gross income*, or *scheduled gross income*, which means the *maximum rental income* at 100 percent occupancy
>   - *effective gross income*, which means the *actual income* after subtracting vacancies and rent collection losses
>   - *net operating income (NOI)*, which is *what's left of the effective gross income after subtracting all of the property's operating expenses*, such as maintenance, taxes, insurance, reserves for replacements, and other recurring expenses (*but not debt service*, such as mortgage interest)

> To *estimate a property value from a cap rate*, an appraiser, licensee, or investor may analyze several recent comparable sales to determine their cap rates, develop an appropriate composite cap rate for the subject property, then *divide the subject property's NOI by the cap rate*.
> - For example, if an analysis determines that a cap rate of 5 percent is what the area market is currently supporting, and the NOI for a property is $100,000, the estimated property value would be $2,000,000.

The **gross rent multiplier (GRM)**, or **gross income multiplier (GIM)** method of estimating value is a simple, informal rule-of-thumb technique that is often used for one-to-four unit residential rentals or small commercial and industrial sites.

Using recent sales, the appraiser, licensee, or investor **divides each comparable property's sales price by its gross income, either monthly or annual**, using the same time-period standard for all, to determine their respective GRMs.

Then, after developing a representative GRM from a reconciliation of the collective GRMs, the appraiser, licensee, or investor **multiplies the subject property's income by the GRM** to arrive at a general estimate of value.

For example, if the appraiser, licensee, or investor develops a GRM of 135 for monthly rents in an area, and is analyzing a property with a monthly rent of $1,200, the property's value would be expected to be around $162,000.

In practice, the income approach is very sensitive to property differences and complexities, highly specialized analysis techniques, and disagreements among appraisers about applications.

The above explanation is intentionally very basic, and repeated here from Topic Area I-C to reinforce a basic exposure to a few terms you may see on the test and some concepts you may encounter soon after becoming licensed.

MATH Questions!!

Property management provides another area for math questions, but probably no more than **between two and four math** questions will be based on topics found in this Topic Area. The questions will provide all the numbers and information necessary to do the math.

The property management math topics are most likely to concentrate on areas that a licensee **might reasonably need to compute to confirm, correct, or supply figures on residential and commercial leases**, or **property management agreements**. These would include, but not be limited to, the following topics

- *rental rates*
- *rent payments and security deposits*
  - *total amounts collected*
  - *amounts returned at the end of the lease*
- *occupancy rates*
- *gross income determinations*
- *property manager's income*
- *property capitalization rate*
- *owner's taxable income*
- *general budget review*

As previously noted, most of the math questions on the test are not particularly complicated. Those that are simply require you to take a deep breath and think a little harder. Chances are that you will be able to at least rule out a few of the answer choices and then be able to make a better-odds guess at whatever's left.

And again, for those of you with math anxiety, one strategy for tackling them is to mark them on your answer sheet as soon as they appear, then move on immediately to the next question.

After answering all of the <u>non-math</u> questions, you can then return to <u>JUST</u> the math questions and work them as a group, doing the ones that look easiest first.

This ends the presentation of key terms and concepts likely to be either tested or used as distractors in this Content Outline area.

II-A. Definitions and Types of Agency

Common law broadly refers to the body of "general" laws that are based on custom, conventions, and case law rather than statutory or civil law. The ***common law of agency*** refers to the category of common law that applies to ***relationships and responsibilities created when one person acts as a representative for another***.

Agency relationships and terminology have been the subject of great discussion and jurisdiction-specific legislation in the United States, and elsewhere, for decades.

*This Content Outline Area provides a broad treatment of agency relationships based on the **common law of agency**. Many of the terms and definitions found in common law have been adopted by many jurisdictions' legislative statutes and administrative policies on agency.*

Under the common law of agency, the definitions of the primary terms that identify the ***parties*** and ***their functions in agency relationships*** include
- ***an agent***, who is authorised to act on behalf of another party (generally the principal) and bind that party by the agent's decisions and actions
- ***a principal***, who grants the authority for another to act on the principal's behalf
- ***a subagent***, who acts as an agent of an agent
- ***a customer***, who is not in an agency relationship with a licensee
- ***a client***, who is in an agency relationship, generally as a principal, with a licensee
- ***an attorney-in-fact***, who is any person, not necessarily a lawyer, who has been granted a ***power of attorney*** to act on behalf of someone else as that person's agent
- ***a proxy***, who is a stand-in for another and has limited, generally very temporary authority; this term can be loosely used to mean agent

*In Bermuda, both **"broker"** and **"agent,"** as used in real estate licensing, refer to "agents" as defined under common law. A Bermuda broker is licensed to enter into agency relationships directly with principals, and an agent is licensed to act as an "agent" of the "agent (broker)," which means as a subagent of the agent regarding principals.*

*These terms became the official "terms of art" in Bermuda with the passage of the **Real Estate Brokers' Licensing Act 2017** in late 2017. Prior to this, a Bermuda broker was known as an "agent," and "salesman" was the term used for current agent licensees. This tidbit of historical usage should help you understand some otherwise confusing terminology in pre-Act contracts and other documentation, not to mention in conversations with your colleagues who have been licensed for a while!*

*Ultimately, though, you should be both familiar and flexible with the evolving nature of these terms. Please note, too, that **throughout this Content Outline Area on Agency, "agent" will refer to anyone acting as an agent in an agency relationship, including brokers, agents, and all subagents**. Further, throughout this Guide, **"licensee" will be used wherever the reference is to*** *generic licensees, both brokers and agents, with **"agent" or "broker/agent" reserved for those situations where that level of licensure and/or authority within a real estate firm is necessary**, such as opening or maintaining trust accounts.*

Types of agency differ depending on the ***extent of an agent's authority***, which ranges from being ***unlimited*** down to being ***specific to one issue or transaction***. The following are ***three broad categories*** of agent authority within agency relationships

1. ***universal***, which grants the agent the authority to ***represent the principal in all matters***; *this may be exemplified by the authority bestowed on someone who has been granted **an unlimited power-of-attorney** for another in both personal and business matters*

2. ***general***, which grants the agent broad authority to ***act continuously on behalf of the principal in all authorised business matters***, such as ***a licensee associated with a broker/agent***, or ***a property manager acting on behalf of a landlord***

   > ***Note:*** *Though* <u>Black's Law Dictionary</u> *identifies this term as synonymous with universal agency, many real estate textbooks distinguish between them, limiting general agency to the range of ongoing responsibilities and authority contained in a particular employer/employee relationship, so look for this distinction in test questions.*

3. ***special***, which means the agent's authority to represent the principal is more restricted than general agency, and typically is ***limited to a particular transaction***, such as ***a listing***

Types of agency relationships vary depending on who the agent represents in a transaction; the most common ***types of agency representation*** and ***terms for the agent*** include

- ***single agency***, which means that the agent is representing only one party, i.e., buyer or seller, in a transaction
  - ***seller's broker***, or ***seller's agent***, which means the type of single agency in which the agent is representing the seller, typically as a listing agent
  - ***buyer's broker***, or ***buyer's agent***, which means the type of single agency in which the agent is representing the buyer
- ***dual agency***, which means the agent is a ***dual agent***, and ***represents both parties***
  > *Note:* <u>disclosure</u> *of dual agency status has always been a good idea, but has become a requirement in an increasing number of jurisdictions.*
- ***subagency***, which means anyone who is authorised to act as an agent for the agent of a principal, in other words, 'below' the primary agent as a ***subagent***

  > *Note: for many decades, many licensees who were working with buyers were <u>technically</u> working <u>for</u> the seller as a subagent of listing brokers through membership in a **multiple listing service (MLS)**.*

  > *To avoid genuine and perceived **conflicts of interest**, various jurisdictions have legislated specific applications of agency law. Some have gone so far as to leave the terms 'subagency/subagent' out of their list of agency relationships to avoid linking it with its former 'automatic' creation. Another approach taken to avoid these situations has the*

broker/agent assign a **designated agent**, or **transaction agent**, to be the only licensee in the office working for a specific client as the broker/agent's subagent.

Regardless of the fine points of these legal considerations, the concept and basic relationship of subagency still survives.

Also, since a licensee acts as a general agent for a particular broker/agent, **when a licensee takes a listing, the licensee is actually creating an agency relationship between the principal and the employing broker/agent.**

The nature of agency relationships, regardless of whether an agent is working for either or both parties in a transaction, requires adhering to a variety of **professional and ethical expectations** that are typically guided by common law **fiduciary duties and responsibilities**.

II-B. Fiduciary Duties

Fiduciary is the term for the trust that marks an agent/principal relationship: **the principal trusts the agent to 'do right.'** But **'doing right' involves** some common legal requirements, obligations, and duties, most notably **the duties of**

- **loyalty**, or **allegiance**, which means to steadfastly work for, never against, the best interests of the principal while applying expected, **reasonable care, skill, and diligence** in the performance of all transaction-related matters
- **obedience**, which means to adhere to the principal's instructions, but **does NOT include illegal actions**
- **accounting**, which means to give a fair and accurate accounting of all funds that are transaction-related, **even if that means after the transaction is over and the agency relationship has been terminated**
- **disclosure**, which means to disclose all pertinent information **to the principal**
- **confidence**, which means to keep confidential all information that might weaken the principal's interests, such as lowest acceptable price or unusual/extenuating circumstances. **Note, though, these conditions regarding confidentiality:**
  - confidential information **may** be revealed **with the principal's permission only**
  - this obligation **does NOT apply to illegal information**, such as **material property conditions**, which **MUST be disclosed** to other parties
  - **confidentiality outlives the termination of the agency relationship**, which means an agent is bound to maintain indefinitely the confidentiality of information acquired in the course of the transaction

A listing **licensee's obligations** include **discussing material property conditions with the owner** and proceeding according to the legal requirements for the particular conditions.

Remember, *material defects must be disclosed*, and *if an owner instructs a licensee to either remain silent or lie about material defects, the licensee cannot legally obey those instructions*, despite the fiduciary duties of obedience and confidentiality.

If this comes up during a listing presentation, and *if the owner insists*, the licensee would be creating an *invalid contract since it would be based on an illegal purpose*, and so *must decline the listing*.

As noted above, the fiduciary responsibility of *confidentiality outlives the termination* of an agency relationship, as does *final accounting* for funds – *this Topic Area is the most likely place to find exam questions on which responsibilities outlast termination of agency, since in practice, it does! So take note!*

As a fiduciary, the agent who accepts earnest money has an obligation of *accounting*, which means the agent is obligated to avoid either of the following situations with transaction-related funds

- *commingling*, which means mingling, or combining, transaction funds with other funds that are required to be maintained separately; this could result from putting the funds in the wrong account, either business or personal
- *conversion*, which refers to *converting funds to another use than the one intended by the principal*, or *misappropriating them*, as in using earnest money to pay office expenses *or for any personal use*; conversion is generally preceded by commingling

*Additional particulars regarding the **handling of earnest money**, such as **to whom it is given**, **into which account it gets deposited**, the **time period within which it must be deposited**, and **method(s) of disbursal, especially when there is a dispute**, are presented in the applicable Bermuda-specific Topic Areas.*

Licensees acting as an agent of a client are legally and ethically bound to adhere to the full range of specific fiduciary duties to that client. Nevertheless, they cannot cheat or lie to others, and in their capacity as a fiduciary to a principal, they also owe the obligations of *honesty and fair dealing* to all parties, including customers.

II-C. Characteristics of Agency Relationships

Characteristics of agency relationships refer to how each type of agency and its fiduciary duties are applied in practice.

Both practical and exam questions from this Topic Area will include *application questions* that *illustrate or explore issues related to the types of agency and fiduciary obligations* defined above, as well as *examples of licensee and broker conduct and obligations to various parties in real estate transactions.*

Some questions are likely to present *examples of licensee conduct* in relation to *principals, clients, customers,* and *members of the public.*

Agency duties would include questions about licensees' *disclosure of any conflict of interest*, such as buying or selling something for themselves, their family, their friends, or their business associates.

Conflict of interest is an especially delicate—and litigious—prospect within any *dual agency relationship*, since a licensee representing both parties has unusual restrictions on every fiduciary duty, most notably loyalty, confidence, and disclosure.

> *By their very nature, **a central characteristic of dual agency relationships** is that they impose obvious **constraints on disclosures of confidential material known about either party**, and conflicts over "full" representation to each arise easily. For example, if a dual agent's keeping the confidence of a seller's motivation from the buyer hurts the buyer's ability to negotiate a lower price, the buyer may feel cheated, perhaps enough to sue.*

> *Some lawyers—and real estate instructors—doubt the basic validity of "dual agency": they argue it is a legal impossibility to act as a true fiduciary for opposing parties. They might even suggest it would be prudent for each party to engage separate lawyers and simply let the "dual agent" licensee play messenger and handle the transaction paperwork. All of this is way too advanced for testing, but illustrates how even "basic" dual agency is anything but simple.*

> *Jurisdictions that formally recognize dual agency have their own legal positions, definitions, guidelines, and regulations. All of these are tied closely to honest and fair dealing, and generally require getting written agreements before sharing sensitive, especially confidential, information. **All exam questions on dual agency on the exam will be based in the broadest application of common law**.*

Another characteristic of an agent's duties in an agency relationship includes recognizing circumstances under which an agent should *refer parties to other professionals* for advice that exceeds the *limits of their professional expertise* and *license authority*.

There are numerous examples in this area, such as referring parties to
- *real estate lawyers* for legal opinions on types of deeds, ways to take title, or property restrictions
- *accountants or tax attorneys* for detailed financial and tax advice
- *surveyors* for property boundary and encroachment questions
- *home inspectors* for detailed property reports
- *appraisers* for property valuation
- *other professionals* as appropriate

For example, in most jurisdictions, real estate sales contracts and many other transaction documents *must* be prepared by attorneys, and then simply used by licensees. In such places, preparing these documents may constitute grounds for *practicing law without a license*.

> *Remember, failure to recommend the appropriate professional could mislead and harm a party, who in turn could take legal action against the licensee.*

Primarily, though, *whenever one party assumes any responsibility for another, that party also assumes obligations to act in the principal's best interests.*

Therefore, any questions, either in practice or on the test, will focus on whether there is, in fact, *(1) an agency relationship*, and if so, *(2) did the agent behave in the best interests of the principal* regarding every aspect of the transaction.

This means performing due diligence in all transaction-related matters, including but not limited to, making ethically and legally appropriate *representations* and *disclosures*, since it is not only expected behavior, but *failure to do so incurs serious liabilities*.

While misunderstandings arise all the time in the course of a transaction, when an agent, or another party, creates them through making representations involving *puffery*, *misrepresentation*, or *fraud*, whenever they are found out, before or after closing, litigation may not be far behind. The basic meaning of these terms includes

- *puffing*, or *puffery*, which refers to any general exaggeration found in promotional materials or agent comments intended to create a stronger impression of a property
- *misrepresentation* means any variety of misleading statements or undisclosed facts that an agent reasonably should have known and disclosed
  - *negligent misrepresentation*, which means making a careless statement where the exercise of due diligence and professional standards of care would have made the correct facts known
  - *material misrepresentation*, which means making a false statement – or failing to make a known, material disclosure – that is likely to induce a reasonable person to act against their own best interest
- *fraud* means intentional misrepresentation designed to persuade a party to make a decision the party would not have made had full and accurate disclosure been made

Where the line is drawn along the scale to distinguish one from the other among these terms, especially between misrepresentation and fraud, is often subjective and settled in court, where it generally rests on degree of knowledge, intent of the party being sued coupled with the degree of injury to the party suffering damages.

A licensee has an obligation to perform a *due diligence property inspection and verification of information* in order to *discover material facts and/or defects* that the *licensee reasonably should have known about*.

Property conditions that are *material*, which means *significant in a party's decision-making process* of approving or disapproving a purchase, *must, when known or reasonably should have been discovered* by a seller, a seller's agent, or even a buyer's agent, *be disclosed*.

> *Material facts* have to do not only with property conditions, but with *any other fact that is significant or essential to a buyer or seller's decision-making process*, even down to types of available financing and date of closing or possession.
>
> *For example, if a buyer needs to move in July 1ˢᵗ but the seller cannot move out until July 15ᵗʰ, that fact is material to the buyer's final decision and must be shared.*
>
> *While this standard of care may extend to* **discovering stigmatizing conditions,** *specific* **disclosures** *regarding cases of a crime, illness, or death on a property***, or are sensitive enough to warrant a current, local legal opinion about how best to proceed.**

This *due diligence* verification also applies to researching and confirming, or correcting, property data supplied by the owner or the owner's agent.

This generally involves reviewing information in *the public record*, such as *assessment data* on *annual taxes*, *lot size and dimensions*, *total square footage of any buildings*, *zoning type and applicable restrictions*, as well as other general property expenses, such as utilities and heating/cooling costs.

Even though an attorney or title company is likely to provide a *title search* in the course of the transaction it is prudent to at least check the ownership/deed records under the name of the "owner."

> *As noted on page 8, a listing licensee in South Carolina was sued by a would-have-been buyer for not having discovered that the "seller" only had a life estate interest in the property. This could have been avoided if the licensee had performed a due-diligence review and either checked the public records or requested, and then read, a title report.*

Due diligence verification can also include matters related to requesting, interpreting, and explaining professional *appraisals*, *surveys*, *home inspections*, *property inspection reports*, or other tests, such as *tests of well water purity*, *soil contamination*, *septic tank condition* and *soil percolation*, or the age, location, and condition of *underground storage tanks* for home heating oil.

Generally, though, questions about material facts will deal with some of the following common types of *material defects*.

> *Material defects* can include
> - *structural physical conditions*, such as a leaky roof, outdated wiring, or foundation cracks

- *structural property environmental problems (internal)*, such as the presence of
  - *wood infestation*, such as termites or other wood-boring insects
  - *lead-based paint*, which is a health hazard, especially to children; *use of lead-based paint was banned in the United States in 1978*
  - *asbestos*, which was widely used for insulation and causes lung problems
  - *drinking water problems*, such as finding unacceptable levels of coliform or e-coli bacteria and/or adverse chemicals in tap water; generally this applies to properties with their own deep or shallow well, or old storage tanks, rather than municipal water
  - *radon gas*, which is a colorless, odorless gas that the Surgeon General of the United States has warned is the second leading cause of lung cancer, arises from the decay of radioactive minerals in the ground and can collect in a basement or other closed areas
  - *urea formaldehyde foam insulation (UFFI)*, which was used extensively in the United States in the late 1970's for wall insulation, and may continue to exude formaldehyde gas, is an irritant and potential cancer-causing agent
  - *toxic mold*, which is becoming an increasingly large problem in recent years; it often infests humid wall spaces and generally spreads unseen
  - *additional toxic problems* that could arise in property inspections, **but should not appear on the test**, include
    - *polychlorinated biphenyls (PCBs), which have been long-banned but were used as coolants and insulators; they are slow to break down and are known to cause liver cancer*
    - *polybrominated diphenyl ethers (PBDEs), which are used in appliances as a flame retardant*
- *property environmental problems (external)*, such as the on-site or nearby presence and effects of
  - *contaminated soil and/or groundwater*, from landfills, chemical discharges, spills, or toxic disposal
  - *underground storage tanks*, which may be deteriorating and/or leaking, and contaminating groundwater supplies
  - *existing or proposed problems*, such as a zoning change allowing a junkyard or landfill area, or a shopping mall creating extra traffic and new patterns

An *agent's obligation* to provide a *due diligence review* to *discover material defects* that the *licensee reasonably should have known about* is an *important characteristic of the professional and ethical expectations* all parties to a transaction have of an agent.

In the event of *nondiscovery or nondisclosure of material facts and/or defects*, the seller and all of the seller's agents, as well as even the buyer's agent, may incur *legal liability and various penalties*, depending on a court's determination of fault.

Liability refers to legal responsibility or accountability. Upon entering into an agency relationship, agents and principals become subject to a wide range of potential liabilities, especially for *willful negligence*, *professional incompetence*, or *unethical conduct*.

Common *types of legal liabilities* include
- *vicarious*, which refers to a *supervisor or principal's responsibility* for the acts of a *subordinate or agent*, respectively; this is most commonly seen in the liability almost any employer has for the professional misdeeds of employees regardless of whether or not they were known to or authorised by the employer
- *joint*, which means *shared liability between two or more parties*
- *several*, which means a *liability of one party that can be legally pursued separately* from other liable parties

An agent as well as a principal can incur legal liabilities for such actions as
- *nondisclosure of property defects* to a party interested in buying a property
- *nondisclosure of environmental hazards* to a party interested in buying a property
- *nondisclosure of other material information* to a party interested in buying a property, such as impending major changes to the neighborhood or immediate area

In addition, an agent can incur legal liabilities for such actions as
- *nondisclosure of agency relationships* to appropriate parties in a transaction
- *lack of due diligence or breach of fiduciary duties*

II-D. Creation and Termination of Agency Relationships

The *creation of agency relationships* occurs in a variety of ways: they may be created by *express* agreements, oral or written, or they may be *implied* by the actions of the parties

An express relationship means that the parties have a *definite oral or actual written mutual understanding* of their representation relationship
- *listing agreements* and *property management agreements* represent the most common examples of *express agency contracts*, since they clearly identify the principal, agent, and their mutual obligations and responsibilities

An implied relationship means that *the actions of the parties suggests there is a representation understanding between them*, as when a licensee and a potential buyer have visited several properties together but have not yet discussed or executed an agency representation agreement
- *family members* and *former clients* represent two categories of potential clients that *create representation misunderstandings through implied agency* – these parties are likely to show up on test questions, and *in practice are best handled with a written representation agreement*

In cases where a licensee is representing a family member, former client, friend, or business associate in a real estate transaction, the most ethical course is to inform all parties, preferably in writing, of the pre-existing relationship. This will also serve to protect the

licensee against legal action for nondisclosure of a potential conflict of interest regarding the seller.

*Terms like **ostensible agency**, or **agency by ratification**, or **agency by estoppel** are types of agency **related to express and implied agency** and **may show up as distractors in test questions**, but are too advanced and legally technical for entry-level testing. However without going into explanations of the nuances that distinguish them from more common types of agency, a quick explanation of each is that*

- **ostensible agency** *is a form of implied agency relationship created by the actions of the parties involved rather than by written agreement, such as the agency relationships that are often automatically assumed to exist (not always correctly) between a licensee and family members*
- **agency by ratification** *is a type of agency, either implied or express, that arises when an unauthorised act by an individual is accepted by the principal after the fact*
- **agency by estoppel** *is a confusing form of agency, often defined during a law suit, by which a third party believes that a certain person is acting as the principal's agent when that person, in fact, is not; also applies to certain situations in which an agent oversteps the actual authority granted by the principal. Generally an agency by estoppel is established when it is determined legally that "mistaken" or unauthorised actions taken are actually binding on the principal due to the principal's allowing misperceptions of delegated authority to go uncorrected.*

An agency relationship is **terminated** for any of a number of reasons, including

- **completion** of the transaction
- **expiration** of the agency period
- **mutual agreement** of the parties
- **breach of contract** by either party, which generally incurs legal liability for the party in breach
- **lack of legal elements** in the original contract, such as finding that the contract was made for an illegal purpose

As noted previously, the fiduciary responsibility of **confidentiality outlives the termination** of an agency relationship, as does the obligation to provide a **final accounting** for funds.

This ends the presentation of key terms and concepts likely to be either tested or used as distractors in this Content Outline area.

III. Powers and Duties of the Superintendent of Real Estate
(5 questions)

This Content Outline Area, as well as Content Outline Areas IV and V, are all based on applicable sections in the ***Real Estate Brokers' Licensing Act 2017 ("The Act")*** and the ***Real Estate Brokers' Licensing Regulations 2017***. Both can be found in their entirety at ***www.BermudaLaws.bm***.

III-A. Powers of the Minister

Under this Act, ***Minister*** refers to ***the Minister responsible for the Registrar of Companies***. Also, the Act accords the following powers to the Minister, all of which may be effected by the Registrar while acting as the Superintendent of Real Estate:

- *licensing authority*
  1. When an application for a licence or renewal of a licence is received and the prescribed fee is paid, the Superintendent of Real Estate, if he is satisfied that the applicant is suitable to be licensed, and is not for any reason objectionable, may grant or renew a licence authorising the holder during the term thereof to carry on the business of a broker or act as an agent in Bermuda.
  2. The Superintendent of Real Estate shall not grant a licence unless he is satisfied that the applicant has met all current minimum criteria for a licence.
  3. The Superintended of Real Estate may revoke a licence where in his opinion such action is warranted by evidence the licensee has actually failed to meet minimum criteria for licensure or has failed to comply with the terms, conditions, or obligations of licensure imposed under this Act.

- *promulgation of regulations*
  1. The Minister ***may make regulations***
     - (a) ***prescribing forms*** for use under this Act and the regulations;
     - (b) ***prescribing the practice and procedure upon an authorised investigation***;
     - (c) ***providing for the examination of applicants for licences***; *the examination is to be set so as to test each applicant's knowledge of the Act and discover if the applicant has the requisite knowledge and skill to practise as a broker in Bermuda;* and
     - (d) generally ***for the better carrying out of the provisions of this Act***, and the more efficient administration thereof.

III-B. Duties of the Superintendent

Under this Act, ***Superintendent of Real Estate*** means the ***Registrar of Companies***, whose duties include requiring, at any time,

- that further information or material be submitted by an applicant or a licensed person within a specified time limit; and
- if the Superintendent so desires, verification by affidavit or otherwise of any information or material then or previously submitted.

III. Powers and Duties of the Superintendent of Real Estate
(5 questions)

In addition, the Superintendent is responsible for administrative details regarding licensing and licensees, including but not limited to overseeing the licence exam, processing all licence-related applications, renewals, and status changes, and receiving all annual broker accounting audits.

More recently, and quite importantly, the Superintendent has also been specifically established *as the supervisory authority for real estate brokers, for the purpose of detecting or preventing*

- *money laundering;*
- *the financing of terrorism; and*
- *the financing of the proliferation of weapons of mass destruction.*

To this end, the Act states that it *shall also be the duty of the Superintendent to keep under review the operations of this Act and developments in the field of real estate that appear to him to be relevant to the exercise of his power and the discharge of his duties.*

In short, everything that falls under the professional activities that would require holding a real estate licence is subject to review and legal action by the Superintendent, and *all Bermuda real estate activities* are subject to his review and possible referral to other authorities.

III-C. Examination of Records/Audit

In order to ensure that the provisions of this Act and any regulations made thereunder are being complied with, or for the purposes of an authorised investigation, the Superintendent or a person authorised by the Superintendent may at reasonable times demand the production of the following documents for the Superintendent's inspection

- all or any of the books mentioned in the next Topic Area; and
- all or any documents relating to a trade in real estate effected by any broker or agent.

A person who has the custody, possession or control of the books or documents requested shall produce and permit the inspection of them by the Superintendent or person authorised by the Superintendent.

Further, a broker shall submit to the Superintendent in each year within the time required a report by the broker's auditors in a form prescribed by the regulations stating that

- the broker has kept proper books and accounts of the broker's trades in real estate;
- the auditor has examined the balances due to clients in trust as at the relevant date in that year, and found them in agreement with the accounting records of the broker;
- the moneys on deposit held in trust for clients has been verified by personal inspection or by certificates obtained from the bank with which the account is maintained;
- the amount due to clients in trust as reflected by the records of the broker, as at the relevant date in that year;
- the auditor has done a sufficient review of the trust account transactions of the broker for the 12-month period immediately preceding the relevant date in that year, to satisfy the auditor that the trust moneys held for clients are kept separate and apart from moneys belonging to the broker; and

- after due consideration the auditor has formed an independent opinion as to the position of the trust moneys held for clients, and to the best of his information the trust moneys held for clients are maintained in a separate trust account and are not less than the amount of trust moneys received in respect of which there is an undischarged trust obligation.

For administrative purposes, it is worth including here that
- an auditor may select as the relevant date either the 30th day of June or the last day of the broker's financial year,
- the report shall be submitted to the Superintendent within six months of the relevant date selected by the auditor, and
- the broker's auditor shall be a person entitled under the Institute of Chartered Accountants of Bermuda Act 1973 to practice as a public accountant.

III-D. Investigations, Notices, and Appeals

Under the Act, *the Superintendent is authorised to conduct investigations* into a wide range of matters related to the real estate practice and licensee conduct in Bermuda. These may be initiated by a complaint to the Superintendent or for routine purposes. Generally, *a licensee or firm* under investigation *is entitled to both a notice and an appeals process*. All of these will be sketched below.

Regarding investigations, the Superintendent, or a person authorised by the Superintendent, may
- on complaint of a person interested, or when the Superintendent deems it necessary without complaint, investigate and enquire into
  1. *any matter concerning the due administration of this Act or any other Act*; or
  2. the circumstances surrounding a transaction or matter or action done by a broker or an agent, whether licensed or not licensed
- for the purpose of such an investigation, enquire into and examine any business or employment to which this Act applies or the person in respect of whom the investigation is being made, and examine and enquire into
  1. books, papers, documents, correspondence, communications, negotiations, transactions, investigations, loans, borrowings and payments to, by, on behalf of, in relation to or connected with the person in respect of whom the investigation is being made; and
  2. property, assets or items owned, acquired or alienated in whole or in part by such person or by a person acting on behalf of or as broker for such person.
- seize and take possession of documents, books, papers, correspondence, communications or records of the person or the business being investigated.

Under the Act, *any person* in respect of whom the investigation is made *shall within five days provide answers to such enquiries*.

In the course of the investigation, the Superintendent may take the following actions regarding *notices* on the matter at hand:

III. Powers and Duties of the Superintendent of Real Estate
(5 questions)

- before making a decision to revoke a licence, the Superintendent shall give the licensee a ***warning notice***, in writing, that states the proposed action and reasons for such action, and allows a specific time of ***at least 14 days for the licensee to provide a response*** for the Superintendent's consideration. At this point, the Superintendent may issue either a ***notice of discontinuance***, in which case the matter is ended, or a ***decision notice***, which means further action is required.
- where the Superintendent considers it proper to issue a ***decision notice***, it appoint an advisory board before which a hearing shall be held
- when the Superintendent issues a ***decision notice***, it ***shall be in writing*** and ***give both the decision and reasons*** supporting the decision, ***and give an indication of the right to appeal the decision to the Supreme Court***
- ***decision notices*** have some particular requirements and purposes, such as
  1. ***they shall be given within 90 days*** of the day the original warning notice was given or else the matter shall be deemed to have been given a notice of discontinuance
  2. they may impose decisions such as
     - ***license revocation***
     - ***a civil penalty***
     - ***public censure, typically a published statement***
     - ***a prohibition order***

A person aggrieved by a decision of the Superintendent ***may be able to appeal to the Supreme Court*** as provided below.

- ***An appeal*** under this section (Act-48) shall lie at the instance of the person aggrieved by the decision of the Superintendent and ***shall be commenced*** by notice of motion filed in the Registry and served on the Attorney-General ***within twenty-one (21) days of the date on which the notice took effect***.

On an appeal, the Supreme Court may confirm, reverse, vary or modify the decision of the Superintendent or may remit the matter to the Superintendent with the opinion of the Supreme Court thereon.

III-E. Offences and Penalties

Under Sections 22 and 49 of the Act, offences are committed whenever a person:
- contravenes a provision of this Act or of any regulations made under this Act;
- omits, refuses or neglects to fulfil, perform, observe or carry out a duty or obligation created or imposed by this Act or any regulation made under this Act; or
- refuses or neglects to produce or permit the inspection of books or documents in the course of an investigation.

There is a ***statute of limitations*** imposed on bringing an action: ***a prosecution under this Act shall be commenced within <u>three years</u> from the date on which the offence is alleged to have been committed***.

III. Powers and Duties of the Superintendent of Real Estate
(5 questions)

Punishment on summary conviction is a *fine of $10,000 or imprisonment for two years, or both*. Further, *penalties for offences* of the Act or regulations *include licence refusal or revocation*.

Finally, the Superintendent has discretionary powers to initiate the refusal or nonrenewal of a licence.

- Section 13 specifies that if the Superintendent *is for any reason of the opinion* that an application for a licence or the renewal of a licence should be refused, he may, in writing, refuse a licence to the applicant.

__This ends the presentation of key terms and concepts likely to be either tested or used as distractors in this Content Outline area.__

This Content Outline Area, as well as Content Outline Areas III and V, are all based on applicable sections in the ***Real Estate Brokers' Licensing Act 2017 ("The Act")*** and the ***Real Estate Brokers' Licensing Regulations 2017***. Both can be found in their entirety at **www.BermudaLaws.bm**.

IV-A.   Activities Requiring a Licence

This Topic Area includes some of the basic definitions of the Act that apply to real estate, the real estate business, and licensing requirements. For example

- ***real estate*** means land in Bermuda, including land covered by water and any building erected on land and any estate, interest, right or easement in or over any land or building in Bermuda
- ***trade***, regardless of whether it is used as a noun or a verb, means:
    1. a disposition or acquisition of or transaction in real estate by sale, purchase, agreement for sale, exchange, option, lease, rental or otherwise;
    2. any offer or attempt to list real estate for the purpose of such disposition, acquisition or transaction referred to above; or
    3. any act, advertisement, conduct or negotiation directly or indirectly in furtherance of such a disposition, acquisition, transaction, offer or attempt
- ***agent*** means a real estate salesman, and includes a person employed by or associated with a broker to trade in real estate
- ***broker*** means a real estate broker, and includes a person who, for another or others, for compensation, gain or reward, or hope or promise of compensation, gain or reward, either alone or through one or more officials or agents, trades in real estate

Simply put, conducting activities that fall under trading as defined above requires a licence, and ***to trade in real estate, one must be licensed as either an agent or a broker***.

The Act specifies that ***no person shall***

- ***trade in real estate*** unless he is licensed as a broker or as an agent of a broker; or
- ***act as an official of or on behalf of a partnership or company in connection with a trade*** in real estate by the partnership or company, unless he or the partnership or company is licensed as a broker; or
- ***act as an agent of or on behalf of a partnership or company in connection with a trade*** in real estate by the partnership or company unless —
    1. he is licensed as an agent of the partnership or company; and
    2. the partnership or company is licensed as a broker
- ***hold himself out as a broker or agent in Bermuda*** unless that person holds a licence under this Act

IV-B. Exemptions

There are exemptions to the licensing requirement, generally for special circumstances, certain professionals, or the buying or selling of property for oneself.

IV. Licensing Requirements   (5 questions)

This Act does not apply to, and licences are not required for, the following individuals
- an assignee, custodian, liquidator, receiver, trustee or other person acting as directed by an Act or under the order of a court, or an administrator of an estate or any executor or trustee selling under the terms of a will, settlement or trust; or
- a person who
  1. acquires real estate in his own name;
  2. disposes of real estate owned by him or in which he has a substantial interest; or
  3. is an official or employee of a person engaged in so acquiring or disposing of real estate in the name of that person

IV-C. Eligibility for Licensing

Eligibility for licensing is relatively straightforward, and this area will also include some of the particulars about licence applications and certain administrative requirements.

In short, *to be eligible for a licence*, an applicant for either an agent or broker licence must demonstrate to the Superintendent that the applicant is
1. *over the age of 18*,
2. either *Bermudian or has permission* from the Minister responsible for Immigration *to work in Bermuda* as a real estate broker, or agent, as the case may be, and
3. *a fit and proper person*, meaning that the person has the requisite probity, competence, and soundness of judgement to provide the professional diligence, prudence, integrity, and skill necessary to protect both the public against loss and the profession against disrepute

Further, the applicant must have passed the written exam as prescribed by the Superintendent

Applications for the grant of a licence as either an agent or a broker *shall be made to the Superintendent* on the prescribed form and accompanied by the current fee.
- *Any applicant for a licence or a renewal of a licence shall provide an address for service in Bermuda.* This requirement allows the Minister or Superintendent to be able to get in direct contact with a licensed agent or broker on any matter of interest regarding the licensee's professional conduct.

There are two extra provisions regarding *the licensing of brokers*
1. *No broker shall be licensed unless he maintains an office in Bermuda* satisfactory to the Superintendent, from which he conducts his real estate business.
2. No person shall be licensed as a broker unless the Superintendent is satisfied after investigation that the person is qualified to be licensed as a broker at the time of his application.

IV-D. Licence Renewal

In Bermuda, *real estate licences expire, or lapse, on September 30th* annually.

To renew a licence each licensee *must apply to the Superintendent* for its renewal
- *on or before the 20th day of September* next after that licence is issued the holder thereof applies for its renewal

- the application for renewal of a licence must be on the proper form and accompanied by the current fee
- *the renewal application requires an address for service in Bermuda*

IV-E. Notice of Change in Licence

Changes in licence include *change of employing broker* or *changes of pertinent information*, such as address for service, which need to be reported in order for an updated licence to be issued.

When an agent has transferred employment from one broker to another broker, it shall be *the duty of both brokers to immediately notify the Superintendent in writing* of that change; the broker that the agent is leaving is required to *return the agent's licence within two business days* to the Superintendent together with a written statement of the reason the agent has left the broker.

A *licensed broker shall immediately notify the Superintendent in writing* of
1. *a change in the address for service*;
2. *a change in the partners* in the case of a partnership; and
3. *the commencement and termination of employment of each agent*.

Note: the last point means *both the former and the new employing broker* have a responsibility to notify the Superintendent of the transfer.

Further, licence changes include revoked, cancelled, or suspended licences.
- Where *a broker's licence* is revoked or suspended that *broker shall within two business days return his licence <u>and the licence of each of his agents</u>* to the Superintendent.
   - Where *an agent's licence* is revoked or suspended *the broker employing or associated with that agent shall within two business days return that agent's licence* to the Superintendent.
- Upon the *termination of the employment or association* of an agent for any reason, *the broker employing or associated with him shall within two business days return that agent's licence* to the Superintendent, together with a written statement of the circumstances of the termination.

<u>This ends the presentation of key terms and concepts likely to be either tested or used as distractors in this Content Outline area.</u>

V. Statutory Requirements Governing the Activities of Licensees
(15 questions)

This Content Outline Area, as well as Content Outline Areas III and IV, are all based on applicable sections in the ***Real Estate Brokers' Licensing Act 2017 ("The Act")*** and the ***Real Estate Brokers' Licensing Regulations 2017***. In addition, the ***Electronic Transactions Act 1999*** has some applicability to the Topics of "Handling of Documents" and "Record Keeping" in this Content Outline Area. All three can be found in their entirety at ***www.BermudaLaws.bm***.

V-A. Advertising

The Act has brief, but very specific guidelines in its section on Regulation of Trading regarding advertising. In short, Section 27 of the Act says that

- when ***advertising*** to ***purchase, sell, exchange, or lease*** any real estate, a broker or agent ***shall clearly indicate*** that ***the licensee is***
  - ***the party advertising*** and
  - ***a real estate broker or agent***, as the case may be

Additionally, the Act requires that ***a reference to the name of an agent*** in the advertisement ***shall clearly indicate that the agent is an associate of the broker***, which means that the employing or associated ***broker is also identified*** in the advertisement.

V-B. Broker/Agent Relationship

All agents are required to operate under the authority of <u>one and only one</u> licensed broker, and ***all licensee remuneration must come from, or be processed through, the licensee's broker.***

According to Section 31 of the Act, ***no agent***
1. ***shall trade in real estate on behalf of a broker other than the broker who***, according to the records of the Superintendent, ***holds his licence***; or
2. is entitled to or ***may accept a commission or other remuneration for trading in real estate from another person, except the broker who holds his licence***

Also, ***an agent cannot obtain, hold, or renew a licence independently*** of having a registered association with a broker. The Act and supporting Regulations specify that
- an agent ***may only be licensed where he is the agent of a broker***, and
- each ***<u>application for a licence</u> of an agent <u>or a renewal thereof</u> shall have attached*** thereto in a form approved by the Superintendent
  - ***a recommendation of the applicant, made by or on behalf of a licensed broker***; and
  - ***a declaration that the applicant, if granted a licence, is to act as an agent employed by or associated with and representing the broker*** making the declaration or on whose behalf the declaration is made
- ***the licence shall be inscribed with the name of the broker*** as principal of the licensee
- ***upon an agent ceasing to be employed*** with a licensed broker ***the licence of the agent shall become void***

And the Act also prohibits brokers from either employing or directly compensating an agent of another broker as well as unlicensed individuals. Section 28 of the Act states that

- *no broker shall*
    1. *employ, permit, or engage the agent of another broker* or an *unlicensed agent* to trade in real estate; or
    2. *pay commission or other remuneration to such an agent*

In the unfortunate circumstance that a firm's broker passes away, the Regulations provide for *an interim proxy to perform as a personal representative* authorised to act on that broker's behalf.

- Where an individual who carries on business as a broker dies, *the Superintendent may grant to his executor or administrator <u>temporary registration as a broker</u> for* a period of *not more than six months* in respect of the business of the deceased broker.
    - Where temporary registration is granted, all agents licensed as agents of that deceased broker at the time of his death shall be deemed to be licensed as agents of such executor or administrator.

V-C. Remuneration

As noted immediately above, *agents may only receive compensation from their own broker*.

There are other provisions in the Act and Regulations regarding remuneration, including

- *no licensed broker or agent shall pay a commission or other fee to an unlicensed person in consideration for furthering a trade in real estate*, and the Act does not allow legal actions to recover compensation by someone without an active licence; the Act says
    - *no action shall be brought for commission or for remuneration* for services in connection with a trade in real estate *unless at the time of rendering the services the person bringing the action was licensed as a broker*
- *commission or other remuneration* payable to a broker in respect of the sale or lease of real estate *shall be on an agreed amount or percentage* of the sale price or lease price
    - *where no agreement as to the amount of commission has been entered into*, *the rate of commission* or other basis or amount of remuneration *shall be that generally prevailing in Bermuda*
- *no action shall be brought to charge a person* by commission or otherwise for services rendered in connection with the sale of real estate *unless*
    - *the contract* upon which recovery is sought in the action or some note or memorandum thereof *<u>is in writing</u> signed by the party to be charged* or by his broker lawfully authorised in writing; *<u>or</u>*
    - *the person sought to be charged*
        1. *has as a result of the services* of a broker employed by him for the purpose, *effected a sale or lease* of real estate or otherwise agreed in writing by either the sale or purchase or listing agreement; *<u>and</u>*

2. *has duly executed a sale and purchase agreement or lease* signed by all necessary parties and delivered it to the purchaser or lessee

In Bermuda, *net listings are prohibited*, and the following will be repeated in Topic Area V-G, Listings. However, since it represents a prohibited compensation arrangement, it is worth clarifying on this Topic Area that *no broker or agent*

- *shall request or enter into an arrangement* for the payment to him of commission or other remuneration *based on the difference between the price at which real estate is listed for sale and the actual sale price* thereof, or
- may *retain a commission or other remuneration* computed on such an arrangement

V-D. Disclosure

Whenever a licensee intends to acquire any interest in Bermuda real estate that the licensee has listed, the licensee must take certain extra steps in the process.

According to Section 30 of the Act, Purchase by Broker or Agent,

- *no broker or agent shall purchase* for himself *either directly or indirectly real estate listed with him for sale*, *nor* shall he *acquire any interest* therein either directly or indirectly, *unless he has disclosed in writing to (1) the Superintendent and (2) the listing owner* complete details of his negotiations for the sale of the said property to another person.

V-E. Handling of Documents

The Act expects all licensees to handle, maintain, and produce on request all of the trade-related documents identified in other Topic Areas, especially III-C and III-D, including but not limited to licences, ledgers, books, papers, correspondence, communications, and transactions.

Of special note here, though, are the provisions in the Act regarding listings that assert a licensee shall provide copies of signed agreements immediately to the appropriate parties.

According to key subsections of Section 34 of the Act

- a broker or agent *immediately after the execution of an agreement to list* with him real estate for sale, exchange, lease, or rent *shall deliver to the person who signed the agreement a true copy thereof*
- *a broker or agent who has secured* from the owner of real estate *a signed acceptance of an offer to sell, purchase, exchange, lease, or rent such real estate,* the broker or agent *shall immediately deliver a true copy of the acceptance to each of the parties to the contract* or their legal representatives

It is worth noting that according to the *Electronic Transactions Act 1999*, many of these documents may have full legal effect even if produced, shared, revised, and "signed" electronically, either entirely from an Internet-linked collection of PCs or by combining hard copy with the use of fax transmittals.

*The details of how the **Electronic Transactions Act 1999** are implemented in real estate transactions are best left to the conventions observed within your particular firm.*

*Also, **there are exclusions placed on electronic versus hard-copy documents and written signatures that apply specifically to "the conveyance of real property or the transfer of any interest in real property"** (section 6(1)(b)). So, even though many records are acceptable and legally enforceable in electronic form, such as contracts, others are not, most notably original deeds; the exclusion would apply to mortgages and leases as well if there are other laws requiring original documents.*

In practice, it is best to work with your firm's legal counsel to determine which documents and records can safely reside in electronic form or must have an original hard-copy version.

V-F. Handling of Moneys

According to the Act, especially Section 23(2) regarding the handling of monies, *every broker shall (1) establish trust accounts for client funds, (2) not commingle them with* any of the broker's *personal funds*, and *(3) keep appropriate ledgers* for each person from whom moneys are received.

The Act stipulates that *a broker shall maintain*
- *an account in a bank* in which he shall deposit moneys that come into his hands in trust for other persons in connection with his business, and *keep such trust moneys separate and apart from moneys belonging to himself* or to the partnership, in the case of a partnership
- *a ledger trust account for each person* from whom moneys are received in trust *in which he shall enter details of the trust moneys received and the disbursements therefrom*

These accounts and ledgers are subject to the periodic audit as outlined in Topic Area III-C.

V-G. Listings

Regarding listings, the Act specifies that
- *an expiration date must be in sole agreements to make them valid*
- *true copies of listings and sales contracts are to be presented immediately to the appropriate parties,*
- *compensation arrangements based on a net listing are prohibited, and*
- *licensees are prohibited from inducing principals to break a listing contract in order to enter into another*

As the Act states each of these in Section 34, *in an agreement to list real estate*
1. a broker or agent *immediately after the execution of <u>an agreement to list</u>* with him real estate for sale, exchange, lease or rent *shall deliver to the person who has signed the agreement a true copy thereof*
2. *no sole agreement* to list real estate for sale, exchange, lease or rental with a broker or agent *is valid unless it is provided in the agreement expires on a date specified therein*

3. where a broker or agent has secured from the owner of real estate *a signed acceptance of an offer* to sell, purchase, exchange, lease or rent such real estate, the broker or agent shall immediately deliver a true copy of the acceptance to each of the parties to the contract or their legal representatives

Further, according to the Act, net listings and compensation based on such arrangements are prohibited.

- *no broker or agent shall request or enter into an arrangement* for the payment to him of commission or other remuneration *based on the difference between the price at which real estate is listed for sale and the actual sale price* thereof

And competing with other licensees by inducing a principal to breach a contact is prohibited by the Act.

- *no broker or agent shall induce a party to a contract* for purchase and sale, or rental of real estate, *to break the contract for the purpose of entering into a contract with another* principal

V-H. Record Keeping

Under the Act, brokers are required to keep account ledgers and produce them for regular audits as well as any investigation requested by the Superintendent.

According to the Act, *a broker shall keep proper books and accounts* of his trades in real estate, and enter in his books and accounts *in respect of each trade*, including information regarding

1. the *nature of the trade*;
2. a *description of the real estate involved* sufficient to identify it;
3. the *true consideration for the trade*;
4. the *names of the parties to the trade*;
5. the *amount of deposit received and a record of the disbursement* thereof; and
6. the *amount of commission or other remuneration and the name of the party paying it*.

Further, records related to the accounts noted in V-F, Handling of Moneys, need to be properly kept and made available for audits and investigations. As a reminder, *every broker shall maintain*

1. *a ledger trust account* for each person from whom moneys are received in trust in which he shall enter details of the trust moneys received and the disbursements therefrom; and
2. *an account in a bank* in which he shall *deposit moneys that come into his hands in trust for other persons* in connection with his business, *and keep such trust moneys separate and apart from moneys belonging to himself* or to the partnership in the case of a partnership.

According to the *Electronic Transactions Act 1999*, many of these documents may be retained electronically as long as the electronic storage meets certain criteria, most notably that *"the information contained in the electronic record is accessible and is capable of retention for subsequent reference"* (section 13(1)(a)).

V. Statutory Requirements Governing the Activities of Licensees
(15 questions)

V-I. Unfair Inducement

Unfair inducement refers to false promises and representations designed to convince a party to enter into an arrangement that may not be proper, ethical, or to the party's ultimate benefit.

Section 26 of the Act specifies that, regarding representations by brokers or agents,
- *no broker or agent shall make a representation* that he or another person will
    1. resell *or in any way guarantee or promise* to resell real estate offered for sale by him;
    2. sell any of the purchaser's real estate; or
    3. procure a mortgage, extension of a mortgage, lease or extension of a lease

However, *the above prohibition does NOT apply to items 2 or 3 if at the time of making the representation, the person making it delivers a letter or electronic copy thereof setting out the representation in clear language to the person to whom the representation is made.*

V-J. Display of Licence

In order to verify for the public that an individual acting as a broker or agent is, in fact, licensed, the Regulations makes the following requirements regarding the location and availability of physical, paper licences for brokers and agents.

- *A licensed <u>broker</u> shall exhibit his licence and keep it exhibited in a prominent place at the address shown thereon*, and
- *a licensed <u>agent</u> shall keep his licence at the office of the broker whom he is employed by or associated with*, and shall, *on being so requested* by any person, *produce his licence for inspection.*

This ends the presentation of key terms and concepts likely to be either tested or used as distractors in this Content Outline area.

VI. General Aspects of Bermuda Property Law   (20 questions)

VI-A. The Development and Planning Act 1974

> The information in this Topic Area is based on the **Development and Planning Act 1974**. For subsequent changes, please review **www.BermudaLaws.bm** for newer Amendments.

The Development and Planning Act 1974 covers matters such as the duty of the Minister of Planning to **survey the entire island** and **prepare development plans at least once every five years** that take into consideration land use, projected population growth, economic base, and transportation and communication needs.

In addition, the Minister's plan may designate **environmental conservation areas** as well as **special study areas** that require closer study before establishing plans, and prepare separate **local plans** for any part of Bermuda that amplifies the Minister's proposal for development and use of particular areas.

The Act also requires permission for any development, which means making almost any sort of change to land or property, or the use of either. **One change that is specifically mentioned is using an external portion of a building for advertising if it has not been an ordinary use already.**

Permission for development and changes granted under the Act **is good for two years from the date the permission is granted.** If the project granted permission has not been begun within this period, the permission expires and must be requested again.

In cases **where a series of approvals is required**, this **two-year period begins on the date of the last matter to be approved**.

For projects that are begun within the two-year period but not completed before the two years expires, the Minister may assess the progress and serve a **"completion notice"** requiring completion within **a stated period, which will be not less than twelve months from the effective date of the notice.**

The **Minister has the authority to return unfinished projects to their original condition**, and **to revoke or modify development plans**. *Particulars related to these matters are complicated and best left to attorneys.*

The Minister or the Development Applications Board may also authorize tree or shrub preservation as well as create designated areas to protect woodlands, agriculture, beaches, caves, animal habitat, and other natural features.

Further, the Minister has **a list of buildings of special architectural or historical interest**, known as **listed buildings**, as well as **historic areas**, **Crown land**, and **community areas** that come under special consideration for planning purposes. *Again, this is an area with a host of administrative definitions and details that are best handled by attorneys, not real estate licensees.*

Since the content outline specifically refers to subdivisions as an area of importance to real estate licensees, it is presented here in its entirety; some commentary will follow.

VI. General Aspects of Bermuda Property Law   (20 questions)

VI-A.   The Development and Planning Act 1974
1.   Part VI – Subdivisions

Meaning of subdivision

35A   In this Act, *"subdivision" means*

(a) *any conveyance of land by way of a deed or transfer*,

(b) the granting, assigning or exercising of a power of appointment with respect to land,

(c) *the mortgaging or charging of land*,

(d) *the entering into of an agreement of sale and purchase of land*, or

(e) the entering into any agreement which has the effect of granting the use of or right in land directly or by entitlement to renewal for a period of twenty-one years or more;

and "person subdividing" shall be construed accordingly.

Planning permission required for subdivision

35B (1) Subject to this section, *planning permission is required for any subdivision of land*.

(2) Planning permission for subdivision of land is not required

(a) where the person subdividing does not retain the fee or the equity of redemption in, or a power or right to grant, assign or exercise a power of appointment with respect to, any land abutting the land that is being subdivided;

(b) where the land or any use of or right therein is being acquired or disposed of by the Government; or

(c) where the land or any use of or right therein is being acquired solely for the purpose of providing a right of way to a statutory undertaker for a transmission line, pipe, or a pipeline and associated works; but in the case mentioned in paragraph (b), a final plan of subdivision shall, on completion of the transaction, be submitted to the Minister by the Minister responsible for the land in question.

(3) Subdivision in contravention of subsection (1) shall not create or convey any interest in land; but this subsection shall not affect an agreement entered into subject to the express condition contained therein that such agreement is to be effective only if planning permission is obtained.

Application for planning permission to subdivide

35C (1) Application may be made in such manner as may be prescribed by the rules for planning permission to subdivide land.

(2) In considering *an application for planning permission under this section*, the Board shall have regard to *such of the following as may be relevant*—

(a) whether the plan conforms to the development plan for the area;

(b) whether the proposed subdivision is premature or necessary in the public interest;

(c) the suitability of the land for the purposes for which it is to be subdivided;

(d) the number, width, location and proposed grades and elevations of roads, and the adequacy thereof, and the roads linking the roads in the proposed subdivision with the established road system in the vicinity, and the adequacy thereof;

(e) the dimensions and shape of any lots of land;

(f) the restrictions or proposed restrictions, if any, on the land, buildings and structures proposed to be erected thereon and the restrictions, if any, on adjoining lands;

(g) the conservation of the visual amenities of the area;

(h) the adequacy of utilities and services;

(i) the area of land, if any, within the subdivision that, exclusive of highways, is to be conveyed or dedicated for public or community purposes.

(3) The Board may impose such conditions on the grant of planning permission as in its opinion are advisable.

(4) Without restricting in any way whatsoever the generality of subsection (3), the Board may, in particular, impose as a condition when the subdivision abuts on an existing road that sufficient land, other than land occupied by buildings or structures, shall be dedicated to provide for the widening of the road to such width as the Board, after consulting with the Minister responsible for public roads, considers necessary.

(5) *Planning permission for the draft plan of subdivision shall expire at the end of the period of three years beginning with the date of its grant*; accordingly, an application for planning permission based on a final plan of subdivision must be submitted within that period.

(6) Part X of this Act shall apply with the necessary modifications in relation to failure to comply with a condition imposed by the Board under subsection (3) or (4) as it applies to failure to comply with any condition subject to which planning permission to develop land was granted.

Registration of planning permission to subdivide

35D (1) When *the Board has granted planning permission based on a final plan of subdivision under section 35C*, the Minister shall register that plan on the register kept under section 22.

(2) *Planning permission by reference to a registered plan of subdivision shall continue to have effect until superseded by the registration under subsection (1) of any subsequent plan* relating to the same land.

(3) But a registered plan of subdivision that indicates details of any planning permission

(a) previously registered under subsection (1), or

(b) deemed by section 5(2) of the Development and Planning Amendment Act 1997 to have been so registered,

shall not have the effect of superseding any such permission.

Certain subdivisions of buildings not to require planning permission

39 *Where* permission to subdivide land would otherwise be required under this Part but *the land to be subdivided consists only of part of a building (and no other land) nothing in this Part shall*

operate so as to require planning permission to be obtained before such subdivision may be effected.

Certain persons not affected by section 35

40 (1) Nothing in section 35B shall prevent the sale of any land ("the land") by a person retaining abutting land where either —

    (a) that person —

        (i) is a trustee, estate representative or mortgagee selling the land within his powers as trustee, estate representative or mortgagee in relation to that land; and

        (ii) retains the abutting land otherwise than in the character of trustee, estate representative or mortgagee, as the case may be, in relation to the land sold; or

    (b) that person's interest in the land is different from his interest in the abutting land; or

    (c) that person's interest in the land is the same as his interest in the abutting land, but another person has an interest in either the land or the abutting land but not both.

(2) In this Part —

"interest", in relation to abutting land, means an interest of a kind described in section 35B(1)(a);

"retain abutting land" means to retain an interest in abutting land; and

"sell", in relation to land, means to convey it or deal with it in any of the other ways mentioned in section 35A, and grammatical variations of "sell", and cognate expressions, shall have corresponding meanings.

The *key points for licensing purposes* of the above *include the need to apply for and receive planning permission for any of the activities identified as <u>subdivision</u>*, especially the transfer or mortgage of property.

The remainder of the Act deals with administrative details and enforcement provisions that are not relevant to the knowledge needed for an entry-level real estate professional. And, even though it would not hurt to be familiar with the entire Act, other professionals would be responsible for helping property owners or prospective buyers address issues like site excavation or other development plans.

VI-B. The Conveyancing Act 1983

The information in this Topic Area is based on the *Conveyancing Act 1983*. For subsequent changes, please review *www.BermudaLaws.bm* for newer Amendments.

Some general questions from the Conveyancing Act may be categorized and tested under Topic Area I-A, Interests in Real Property. But some that are specific to Bermuda will be considered as part of this outline Topic Area.

According to the common law statute of frauds, all real estate contracts have to be in writing to be legally enforceable except leases for less than a year. Bermuda's Conveyancing Act makes this common law principle true for *real estate sales contracts, which must be signed by the party to be charged*, while extending *the legal validity* of *oral leases* to periods *of up to three years*.

The Act also points out that *leases with options to renew* that would increase the tenancy to three years or more *must be in writing to be legally enforceable*.

Further, the Act provides details regarding (1) *the language required in deeds*, (2) *who may hold original documents*, and (3) *acknowledgements*, which in the Act means a promise to a party to produce those documents on request, with costs involved paid by the requesting party.

Generally the vendor passes all title documents to the purchaser. However, *the vendor is entitled to retain documents of title in cases where the vendor retains any part of the land* to which the documents relate, or the document consists of a trust instrument or instrument creating a trust.

According to the Act, *ownership records only have to go back twenty years*, and *leases for more than twenty-one years may entitle the lessee to a freehold, fee simple interest in the property*.

In addition, *the Act specifically identifies implied covenants for property conveyance documents*, including sales, mortgages, and leases. Some of *these include the covenants of seisin, quiet enjoyment, and further assurance* (see Section I-D, Contracts, for definitions), though in Bermuda the *expenses related to providing proof of clear, unencumbered title become the responsibility of the person requesting the proof*.

The particulars of these covenants and conveyance documents are best addressed by the attorneys who prepare the documents, not by real estate licensees.

An important provision in the Act is Section 27, *which obligates a lender to accept mortgage assignments and any associated property ownership conveyance*.

The Act also spells out the rights and conditions under which a lender may exercise a power of sale, and the fact that *a mortgagee cannot insure, or require insurance, in excess of either the loan amount or the replacement value of the property*.

Another important element of the Act is that *all voluntary conveyances must be deposited with the Registrar General for registration and recordation within thirty days of having been duly stamped in accordance with the Stamp Duties Act*. The conveyance is to be *accompanied by a memorandum, signed by or on behalf of the grantor(s) and grantee(s)* containing (1) the *date of the conveyance*, (2) the *names of the parties*, and (3) a *property description*.

And the Act also ensures that *any party* to a property-related transaction *has the right to appoint an attorney of their own choosing,* and cannot be restricted to relying on an attorney designated by any other party—*any stipulation* that restricts a party's right in this matter *is void*.

VI-C. The Land Valuation and Tax Act 1967

> The information in this Topic Area is based on the *Land Valuation and Tax Act 1967* and *Land Tax Act 1967* and reflects applicable amendments from the *Land Tax Amendment Acts of 2002, 2004, 2010, 2013, 2016, 2019, and 2023* and the *Land Valuation (Reorganization) Act 2002*. For subsequent changes, please review **www.BermudaLaws.bm** for newer Amendments.

According to the Act, the *annual rental value (ARV)* is defined as "the rent at which *a valuation unit* might reasonably be expected to let from year to year *if the tenant undertook to bear the cost of internal repairs*, and *the landlord to bear all other reasonable expenses necessary to maintain the valuation unit* in a state to command that rent, *but excluding any element attributable to any tax payable under this Act*."

The Act defines *an owner, or "tax payer," of a valuation unit* to include *not only the person who is entitled to receive rental monies*, but *the occupier* in the case of (1) *a rental for a period greater than three years*, (2) *a life tenancy*, or (3) *Crown land*.

The Act also defines *tax period* to mean the *semi-annual periods* between *January 1st and June 30th* and *July 1st to December 31st*.

The *Director of Land Valuation*, or *Director*, who is appointed by the Governor, *has the responsibility of establishing the ARVs of all valuation units in Bermuda that fall under the authority of the Act*.

Some properties are *exempt from the Act*, including (1) *properties owned <u>and</u> occupied by the Crown*, (2) domestic and foreign government buildings, (3) charitable organizations, (4) schools, (5) homes of clergymen, and (6) day care centres.

The Director endeavours to be fair in the equitable assignment of ARVs in the draft list. The list sets out (1) the ARV of each valuation unit, (2) the location of the unit, and both (3) the reputed owner and (4) the actual occupier.

Under Bermuda law, *anyone contacted for property information by the Director must respond within twenty-one days or be subject to penalties for failure to comply*.

Further, the Director or someone acting under the Officer's authority *may expect to gain access to a property by giving at least twenty-four hours' written notice of a request to enter, survey, and value a valuation unit*. Anyone who wilfully delays or obstructs this request is subject to penalties.

The draft valuation *list has to be updated on a quinquennial, or five-year, cycle* and be *made available at every Post Office as well as the Director's office*. Once the required notice that the list has been prepared and circulated to each Post Office, *the list must remain available for public inspection for at least one hundred and eighty days*.

In the event a person feels a property's listed ARV is incorrect or unfair, *there are provisions for objecting and appealing the list's information*; these must be *made in writing*, and have some quite specific and administrative requirements, so will not be summarized here. However, that there are provisions to address problems is important to know.

The Tax Commissioner charges, levies, and collects taxes half-yearly, though taxes *may be paid at the office of the Accountant General*. *All taxes* collected *are paid into the Consolidated Fund.*

The Tax Commissioner may also act *to collect on unpaid taxes by distrain, or taking personal property*, as well as *garnishing wages, salary, or pension.*

According to the Land Tax Amendment Acts of 2004, 2010, 2013, 2016, and 2023, the Tax Schedule related to the Land Valuation and Tax Act 1967, referred to as the Principal Act, is as follows:

Land Tax on Private Dwellings

Annual Rental Value Band	$ Value	Rate of Tax -- %
1	0 – 11,000	0.8
2	11,001 – 22,000	1.8
3	22,001 – 33,000	3.5
4	33,001 – 44,000	6.5
5	44,001 – 90,000	17.0
6	90,001 – 120,000	35.0
7	120,001+	55.0

Any calculation questions on the exam will be based on the most recent figures applicable; please check www.BermudaLaws.bm for the most recent version of the Land Tax Amendment Act.

VI-D. The Stamp Duties Act 1976

The information in this Topic Area is based on the *Stamp Duties Act 1976* and reflects applicable amendments from the *Stamp Duties Amendment Acts of 1999, 2000, 2001, 2005, 2008, 2019, and 2023*. Please review *www.BermudaLaws.bm* for newer Amendments.

The Stamp Duties Act 1976 is lengthy (approximately 75 pages), complex, and applies to far more than real estate transactions.

A few general points about the Act include:
- any instrument executed outside Bermuda that would be subject to stamp duty in Bermuda will neither be valid in Bermuda nor registered in Bermuda unless it is duly stamped
- there is a Schedule for time-after-execution for proper stamping of certain documents, which commences the day after the execution of the instrument in question by the person who last executes it; however, certain documents must be stamped before execution
- stamps are placed by either adhesive stamps, properly canceled, or a franking machine
- no instrument chargeable with stamp duty shall be acted upon, filed, or registered without it
- whenever any stamp duty is payable in respect of a conveyance or transfer of property, the Accountant General may ascertain the value of such property in a manner as he thinks fit
- there are provisions that establish allowances for spoiled stamps

VI-D. The Stamp Duties Act 1976
1. Conveyance and Transfer

Conveyance and transfer considerations are in Part VII, Conveyances, of the Stamp Duties Act. The key points of this area as they relate to real estate include, often in very convoluted language,

- when property is conveyed for consideration, the conveyance is chargeable with ad valorem duty
- special considerations affecting the amount of stamp duty chargeable on the conveyance from a sale include pro rata consideration among multiple purchasers, if applicable
- where a purchaser has not yet obtained a conveyance but sells the property, or its equitable interest, to another, the ad valorem duty is based on the price paid by the third party
- in the event a purchase doesn't go through after ad valorem duty has been paid, it shall be returned

According to the Schedule, Heads 14 and 15, the stamp duty for the conveyance or transfer of Bermuda property is, as of the Stamp Duties Amendment Act 2023, as follows, unless exempted:

1. 2.10% on the first $100,000 or any part thereof
2. 3.15% on the next $400,000 or any part thereof
3. 4.20% on the next $500,000 or any part thereof
4. 6.30% on the next $500,000 or any part thereof
5. 7.35% of all amounts over $1,500,000

VI-D. The Stamp Duties Act 1976
2. Appraisements

According to the Act, Section 65, any person by whom an appraisement or valuation chargeable with stamp duty is made commits an offense if:

- within fourteen days after the making thereof neglects or omits to write out the same in words and figures showing the full amount thereof on duly stamped paper, or
- in any other manner discloses the amount of appraisement or valuation

The latter applies to improper attempts to make an official document for the appraisement.

And, according to the Schedule, Head 8, the stamp duty is either $27 or ¼% of appraisements that do not exceed $10,000, payable by the appraiser.

VI-D. The Stamp Duties Act 1976
3. Leases

According to the Act, Section 59, where any financial consideration of a lease entails the lessee to erect a building or otherwise add to improvements, the amount contributed to the property improvements is considered a premium and charged with ad valorem duty.

VI. General Aspects of Bermuda Property Law   (20 questions)

And, according to the Schedule as shown in the Stamp Duties Act 1976 and amendments to Head 25 of the Stamp Duties Amendment Act 2019, within 30 days after execution of a lease the following stamp duty is due on the respective monthly rental amounts:

Term of Lease	Duty
1. Up to three years	1.05% of the aggregate rent payable for the term of the lease
2. More than three years	1.05% of the aggregate rent payable for the first three years of the lease, plus 0.5% of the aggregate rent payable for any additional period beyond three years

VI-D. The Stamp Duties Act 1976
4.   Mortgages

According to the Stamp Duties Act 1976 and the Stamp Duties Amendment Act 2005, Head 31, within 30 days after execution of a mortgage, the following stamp duty is due on the more common types of mortgages:

1. .25% of the principal sum for a primary mortgage of $400,000 or less; .5% if more
2. .10% of the sum for a secondary mortgage
3. .25% of the sum on an equitable mortgage of $400,000 or less; .5% if more

VI-E. The Rent Increases (Domestic Premises) Control Act 1978

The information in this Topic Area is based on the *Rent Increases (Domestic Premises) Control Act 1978* and reflects applicable amendments from the *Rent Increases (Domestic Premises) Control Amendment Acts of 2000, 2004, 2009, and 2016*. Please review *www.BermudaLaws.bm* for newer Amendments.

Under this Act, the following *definitions* are particularly noteworthy
- *domestic tenancy means a tenancy of premises let as a dwelling*
- *domestic tenancies* subject to the provisions of this Act *do NOT include*
  - *dwellings on agricultural land* occupied by persons working the land
  - *tenancies for a life or lives*
  - *boarding or rooming houses*
  - *tenancies not exceeding twelve months of a house in which the landlord ordinarily resides*, but is temporarily *out of Bermuda*
  - *tenancy of any premises with an annual rental value in excess of $22,800* (per the 2016 Amendment Act)
- *landlord* includes *any person*, other than a mere collector, *who receives rent*, whether on his own account or as an agent for another; also, relating to a particular tenant, the person entitled to receive rent from that tenant
- *tenant or sub-tenant* includes (1) *a person in possession* of premises subject to this Act, and (2) *a person who retains possession* of any premises by virtue of this Act
- *"tenancy" includes sub-tenancy* as well as primary tenancy

- *premium* refers to *consideration collected in addition to rent*, such as fines, other sums, or other valuable consideration
- *Commissioner* means the person appointed under this Act to carry out the Act

Where disputes arise over whether the use of a premises is domestic and therefore subject to the provisions of this Act, there are guidelines for applying to the Commissioner for a certificate as to the use; the guidelines are too administrative to apply to entry-level practice.

Licensing of tourist accommodations are similarly regulated, and a licence will be revoked if a premises is let for more than an aggregate of six months in any consecutive twelve-month period to a person who is ordinarily resident or employed in Bermuda.

For tenancies subject to this Act, in the absence of a written clause, the Act creates an implicit covenant that *if rent payment is not received within 15 days of the due date the landlord has cause for forfeiture.*

There are a variety of conditions governing the continuation and termination of tenancies, such as protections for a tenant's surviving spouse and/or resident family members against terminations, and to allow landlords to regain possession for family use.

These are complex issues, and generally require the interested party serving a notice to quit to the party in possession, the latter serving a counter notice on the first party, and then the first party applying to the court for an order for possession of the premises.

Though such matters as those above are important, they are properly handled by an attorney or by other experienced professional, not by an entry-level licensee.

However, it is worth knowing that *the Act specifically allows a notice to quit to take effect as if the Act had not been enacted when the tenant is* determined to be *an "undesirable tenant,"* which means the tenant
- *uses the premises for any illegal purpose*, or
- persistently *admits to the premises any person of bad character*, or
- *causes unnecessary annoyance, disturbance, or damage* to the landlord or the property or other persons, or
- *breaches the agreement*, especially through *persistently being more than two weeks behind in rent;*
  - *at the time of serving notice to quit for nonpayment, the rent must be at least two months in arrears*

Increases in rents are generally arranged either
1. *by an agreement with the tenant* or
2. *through an application to and grant of certificate from the Commissioner*

When the increase comes by an *agreement with the tenant*, a few conditions apply
- the *landlord shall lodge proper notice* of the increase *with the Commissioner* who in turn shall endorse it and return a copy to both the landlord and the tenant
- the *increase shall not be the result of the landlord's requiring it as a condition of continued or renewed tenancy*; *any such arrangement is illegal and void*
- the Commissioner may refuse to endorse any agreement he believes is illegal until he is satisfied it is valid;
  - he may make such enquiries as necessary to determine that there is no infringement of the Act and that the tenant is familiar with the rights granted under the Act
  - he shall notify the landlord in writing of such enquiries

When the landlord *applies for a rent increase* to the Commissioner, the Commissioner shall serve a copy on the tenant, who then has 14 days to return comments regarding the increase to the Commissioner.

The Commissioner, either upon receipt of the tenant's comments or after a month of serving the landlord's request on the tenant, shall determine that the increase is either
- reasonable, and serve the landlord and tenant certificates stating a fair increase that shall not exceed the increase requested, or
- not reasonable, and serve the landlord and tenant certificates stating his comments regarding the request

The landlord or the tenant is allowed to respond to either certificate and appeal to the court if the Commissioner's response isn't mutually satisfactory, but the process from here becomes too administrative to warrant further summary.

What is important for entry-level licensees to know is how it gets started and that there is a continuing process open to each party to get the Commissioner and other authorities to reconsider decisions regarding rent increases.

Further, though there are provisions stipulating that new tenancies have rent increase limitations that cannot exceed the rent paid, or increase approved, of the last tenancy. However, these are not an entry-level licensee's concern. Brokers or lawyers—and eventually, but not now, you—will be responsible for ferreting out the details of such things, so they won't be summarized here.

Key money is prohibited. This term, and prohibition against it, applies to any premium, including but not limited to the purchase and leaving of furniture in excess of rental value, required as for the grant, renewal, continuance, or assignment of a tenancy.

A landlord may, though, require a deposit of an amount *not exceeding the greater of a fortnight's rent or $100*, providing that *the amount is to be refunded in its entirety unless there are legitimate deductions* due the landlord based on tenant damages.

Any person who violates these provisions regarding key money is subject to penalties that could include imprisonment and/or fines.

VI-F. The Bermuda Immigration and Protection Act 1956

The information in this Topic Area is based on the ***Bermuda Immigration and Protection Act 1956*** and reflects applicable amendments from the ***Bermuda Immigration and Protection Amendment Acts of 2002, 2003, and 2007*** as well as the ***Policy Statement and Notes for the Acquisition of Residential Property by Non-Bermudians as Amended in 2003, 2005, and 2006***. Please review ***www.BermudaLaws.bm*** for newer Amendments.

The Bermuda Immigration and Protection Act 1956 has extensive provisions and subsequent amendments *governing which individuals are entitled to Bermudian status*.

The particulars of who is or is not Bermudian, how they acquired or lost Bermudian status, and the rights of Bermudians is of little significance to real estate licensees beyond knowing that

- *Bermudians have certain rights* regarding the acquisition and use of Bermuda real estate that are not available to non-Bermudians
- *non-Bermudians are subject to specific restrictions* regarding the acquisition and use of Bermuda real estate, and are referred to in the Act as *restricted persons*
- *Bermudian status may be extended* to certain long-term residents, spouses, parents, and/or siblings of Bermudians, and select other individuals
- *the Minister responsible for immigration is authorised to grant individuals who qualify a <u>certificate</u> attesting to their Bermudian status, and to revoke same*
- *restricted persons who acquire land* by means such as inheritance or foreclosure *may either be granted a <u>licence</u> by the Governor* to hold it *or be required to sell it*, generally *within three years* of its acquisition

When working with a party on a real estate transaction, it is best to leave the determination and verification of Bermudian/non-Bermudian status to the proper authorities. Nevertheless, depending on the transaction, it could save everyone involved a lot of trouble and expense to verify the party's certificate of Bermudian status earlier rather than later in the process.

VI-F. The Bermuda Immigration and Protection Act 1956
1. Policy Statement and Notes for the Acquisition of Residential Property by Non-Bermudians

Important Note: *The material presented below is current as of the Policy as amended 26 April 2016; the ARVs there can be found in the **Bermuda Immigration and Protection (Minimum Annual Rental Values) Regulations 2007** and **Bermuda Immigration and Protection (Minimum Annual Rental Values) Amendment Regulations 2012 and 2016**. <u>If there are subsequent amendments, the exam will reflect applicable changes</u> and will not include conflicts between the below and any updates.*

The introduction of the Policy Statement, which seeks to curtail non-Bermudian property speculation afforded through non-personal-use ownership, specifically states

VI. General Aspects of Bermuda Property Law   (20 questions)

- The underlying philosophy of the policy is to preserve the majority of the housing stock and undeveloped residential land for Bermudian ownership. It is recognised that *there is only a small Bermudian market for the highest priced houses and that these may be acquired by non-Bermudians for their own private residential use*.

Some of the main points of the policy that are of interest to more commonplace real estate transactions include

- *non-Bermudians* wishing to acquire property in Bermuda *are required to obtain a licence* from the Minister of Labour, Home Affairs & Public Safety
  - *a non-Bermudian* can acquire *a house ONLY if the property has an Annual Rental Value (ARV) of $126,000 or more*, however
    - *permanent residents* can acquire a *house as long as its ARV is $63,600 or more*
    - ordinarily, *multi-unit properties* cannot be acquired by a non-Bermudian, *except for properties already owned by a non-Bermudian*. In such cases, at least *one unit must have an ARV at or above the minimum ARV required at the time of application, currently $126,000.*
  - *a non-Bermudian* can acquire *a condominium or apartment ONLY if it has an ARV of $25,800 or more*

VI-G. The Landlord and Tenant Act 1974

The information in this Topic Area is based on the *Landlord and Tenant Act 1974*. Please review *www.BermudaLaws.bm* for newer Amendments.

Under this Act, there are several requirements and provisions that real estate licensees may encounter in the course of business related to residential tenancies, including

- a *contract of tenancy* means any lease or tenancy agreement
- under an *oral lease*, there is an *implied agreement to pay the rent monthly in advance*

Landlords have certain *repair obligations* for *short residential tenancies*, meaning *tenancies for terms less than three years*, as *implied covenants* regardless of whether the lease is oral or written.

Also, there is an *implied covenant that the landlord or authorised agent may enter the premises* to view its condition and state of repair, *provided that written notice is given to the tenant at least twenty-four hours in advance and entry is made at reasonable times of the day*.

The landlord is specifically required to keep the following in repair

- the *structure and exterior* of the house or apartment, *including drains, fresh water tanks, and external pipe*
- any *cesspool* connected to the dwelling
- *installation*s for the supply of water, electricity, gas (if any), and sanitation, i.e., basins, sinks, baths, and showers (but not fixtures and fittings), and heating water, if already installed
- the above *landlord's repairing covenant* does NOT apply to
  - (1) repairs necessitated by tenant destruction or misuse,

(2) destruction due to fire, tempest, flood, or other inevitable accident,

(3) anything that the tenant is entitled to remove from the dwelling

- unless the court authorises a modification to the contrary, *any agreements that attempt to exclude or limit the above covenants or agreements are void*

Tenants have certain covenants that are *implied in the absence of an agreement*, and that are *implied in written agreements* unless specifically addressed otherwise. These include

- *paying the rent monthly in advance*
- *paying for electricity*
- *paying for any gas used*
- *using the premises only as a private dwelling*
- *neither assigning nor subletting the lease* nor *making any alterations* to the premises *without the written consent of the landlord or landlord's agent*
- *performing routine minor maintenance tasks*, such as replacing tap washers, fuses, window panes, screens, and door keys
- *delivering the premises in a clean and proper condition* at the end of the lease period

Termination provisions generally observe the following guidelines

- *a contract of tenancy for a specific period* of time *terminates without notice when the period ends*
- *tenancies from year to year* shall be terminated by *not less than six months' previous notice* given at any time *after the end of the first year of the tenancy*
- *tenancies for successive periods* of *more than a month and less than a ye*ar shall be terminated by *notice not shorter than the rental period given at any time after the end of the first rental period*
- *tenancies for successive periods* of a *month or less* shall be terminated at the end of the rental period by *not less than one month's previous notice*
- *a contract of tenancy terminable on notice* by either party *terminates on the expiration of notice duly given, which means*
    - *notice to terminate* a tenancy *shall be in writing*
    - *termination notice shall* either *be personally delivered to the respective party* or *served on the respective party in the manner prescribed in the Act*

When *either a landlord or tenant* seeks to *terminate a tenancy based on breaches of the other's obligations*, the respective party may *apply to the court for an order to terminate the contract of tenancy*.

*These matters are detailed and administrative, and complicated beyond an entry-level licensee's need to know. However, it is worth knowing that there is a court process to address termination disputes, and that generally **the tenancy continues and rights and obligations of parties remain enforceable unless and until the court makes an order**.*

VI. General Aspects of Bermuda Property Law   (20 questions)

According to the Act, when a premises has not been vacated, *a landlord shall be entitled to compensation* for the use and occupation of the premises.

This compensation does NOT allow a landlord to *distrain*, or seize a tenant's property, for rent due; any provision in a contract allowing this action shall have no force or effect.

Also, if the landlord accepts compensation or past rent after the expiration of a tenancy or notice or order for the termination has been made, *such acceptance does not operate as a waiver of the notice or a reinstatement or creation of a tenancy*, unless the parties so agree.

VI-H. The Human Rights Act 1981

The information in this Topic Area is based on the *Human Rights Act 1981* and reflects applicable amendments from the *Human Rights Amendment Acts of 2000, 2013, and 2016*. Please review *www.BermudaLaws.bm* for newer Amendments.

The *Human Rights Act 1981* opens with the following statement, which is reproduced here to clarify the governing philosophy of the Act: all provisions are consistent with the intent expressed.

> WHEREAS recognition of the inherent dignity and the equal and inalienable rights of all members of the human family is the foundation of freedom, justice and peace in the World and is in accord with the Universal Declaration of Human Rights as proclaimed by the United Nations: and

> WHEREAS the European Convention on Human Rights applies to Bermuda: and

> WHEREAS the Constitution of Bermuda enshrines the fundamental rights and freedoms of every person whatever his race, place of origin, political opinions, colour, creed or sex, but subject to respect for the rights and freedom of others and for the public interest: and

> WHEREAS these rights have been confirmed by a number of enactments of the Legislature: and

> WHEREAS it is expedient to make better provisions to affirm these rights and freedoms and to protect the rights of all members of the Community . . .

Under the Act, the following definitions apply
- *the Community* means all persons lawfully residing in Bermuda
- *class of persons* means a class of persons based on one or more of the following criteria
    1. *race*
    2. *place of origin, <u>including Bermuda</u>*
    3. *colour*
    4. *ethnic or national origins*

5. *sex or sexual orientation*
6. *marital status*
7. *disability*
8. *family status*
9. *religion or beliefs*
10. *political opinions*
11. *criminal record, except where there are valid reasons relevant to the nature of the particular offence for which he is convicted that would justify the difference in treatment*

- *disabled person* means a person who has any degree of physical disability, infirmity, malformation, or disfigurement that is caused by bodily injury, birth defect or illness, including diabetes, epilepsy, acquired immune deficiency syndrome, human immunodeficiency virus, paralysis, amputation, lack of physical coordination, blindness or visual impediment, deafness or hearing impediment, muteness or speech impediment, or physical reliance on a guide dog, wheelchair or other remedial appliance or device. *It also means* a person who has, or has had, a mental impairment and the impairment has, or has had, a substantial and long-term adverse effect on that person's ability to carry out normal day-to-day activities.

- *the Minister* means the Minister responsible for the Human Rights Commission

- *discrimination* is determined by whether one person acts toward another person, who happens to be *a member of one of the classes of persons above*, in any of the following ways due to that person's being in one of those classes
  - *treats another less favoubly* than he treats or would treat other persons generally
  - *refuses or deliberately omits to enter into any contract or arrangement* with another on the like terms and the like circumstances as in the case of other persons generally
  - *deliberately treats another differently* than other persons generally

The accumulated provisions of the Act include prohibiting discrimination in the *sale, rental, or advertising* of not only residential property, but business, trade, and all properties for other purposes.

Of special note under the Act are the following conditions as they apply to the classes of people identified above
- *no person shall discriminate against any person who is*
  - *seeking to acquire* any accommodation, premises or other land
  - *occupying* any accommodation, premises or other land
  - *in need of* any accommodation, premises or other land

However, there are certain *exemptions to what constitutes discrimination*, such as
- *members of the opposite sex* may be legally barred from tenancy if the whole residency is, or all rooms in a single housing accommodation are, legitimately restricted to individuals of the same sex
- *owner or family-member <u>occupied</u> residences*, are not subject to the Act it the property
  - *is a single housing accommodation* renting rooms in the family's home

- is a building that contains accommodations for *not more than three families living independently*, if the owner or family members occupy one such accommodation

Though the authority of the Act extends to several other areas, as it directly affects the real estate business, the Act is reflected in its application to *employers and professional organizations*.

Basically, *neither is allowed to discriminate* based on the classes of people above in recruiting, company employment or organization membership, or compensation.

Further, *contract provisions that attempt to circumvent any of the Act's provisions are legally void* in any attempt to enforce them, and there are *penalties for violations* that *begin with fines of $5,000 and escalate to fines of $15,000 and/or three years of imprisonment* for subsequent offences.

__This ends the presentation of key terms and concepts likely to be either tested or used as distractors in this Content Outline area.__

A Few Test-Taking Tips

The exam-prep power of each sample question will be multiplied as much as four-fold if you make sure you know the meaning of the wrong answers, or *distractors*, as well as the correct one.

Distractors are generally written using
- terms and concepts from the same category as the correct answer
- common misconceptions or misunderstandings
- information that is either incomplete, overly complete, or correct for a different, closely-related term.

So remember – when reading the questions, and *especially when reviewing your answers*, pay special attention to the distractors: *Many of them will be used as the "real" answers on the real exam!*

Some of the points made regarding math questions in Content Outline Area I are true for all questions, such as
- *"Mark" any question you need to spend time on, leaving its answer choices blank, then come back to it*
- *Leave no question unanswered: pure guessing gives you 1 out of 4 odds*
  - *However, you should be able to at least rule out a few of the answer choices and then be able to make a better-odds guess at whatever's left*

<u>Finally, remember these Math-specific points as you go into the test</u>

- *If you miss <u>all and only</u> the math questions, you would score 90% or higher on the test*
- *Most of the five-to-ten math questions on the test are not particularly complicated*
  - *Those that are simply require you to take a deep breath and think a little harder*
- *Expect the questions themselves to provide all the numbers and information necessary to do the math*
- *Math questions will use "None of the above" as the fourth choice as a way of verifying that you can calculate the correct answer rather than just work each option backwards or keep trying until your answer matches or gets 'close enough' to one of the choices*
  - *This testing strategy requires you to be confident in your calculations*
  - *Just like with any other question, the "None of the above" option is likely to correct approximately 25% of the time, so if you are confident your answer is not listed, choose that final option*

After completing and scoring the following questions, remember that even if your scores are strong, you should review <u>all</u> of the questions to make sure you also understand the terms and concepts presented as distractors.

100 <u>Now get out that scratch paper, take a deep breath, and begin answering the following questions. Good Luck!</u>

1. The type of legal description that refers to a point of beginning and then uses distances and compass directions is
   A. lot and block.
   B. metes and bounds.
   C. vertical land description.
   D. government rectangular system.

2. During an appraisal of a residential property, an appraiser estimates the cost of rebuilding the subject property so that it is identical to its current size and condition. This is an example of which of the following appraisal principles?
   A. Balance
   B. Conformity
   C. Substitution
   D. Anticipation

3. In order to be valid and enforceable, which of the following elements MUST be part of a deed for the sale of real estate?
   A. A tax assessment
   B. Zoning restrictions
   C. Covenant of seisin
   D. Delivery and acceptance

4. Which of the following property liens would be paid FIRST at the time a property is sold?
   A. Tax
   B. Mechanic's
   C. First mortgage
   D. Special assessment

5. Which of the following types of agency relationship is MOST likely to be created by a listing agreement?
   A. Implied
   B. Special
   C. General
   D. Universal

6. Which of the following types of contract clauses may a lender include in a loan agreement in order to call the entire remaining loan balance due if the property is sold?
   A. Escalator
   B. Alienation
   C. Defeasance
   D. Assumption

3. Which of the following documents creates and identifies the extent of authority for a property manager acting on behalf of an owner?
   A. Licence law
   B. Local zoning laws
   C. Management agreement
   D. The Human Rights Act 1981

8. Which of the following situations BEST exemplifies what is meant by "conversion of funds"?
   A. Depositing an earnest money check in an office account
   B. Using client funds as a source for temporary personal loans
   C. Disbursing office funds from an operating account to cover routine expenses
   D. Transferring money from an account at a listing office to one at the selling office

9. A property manager whose compensation arrangement specifies 50% of the first month's rent up front plus a commission of 10% per month for the remainder of the year's contract has just rented a small warehouse for $9,750 per year. What will the property manager receive in the first year for renting this property?
   A. $ 893.75
   B. $ 975.00
   C. $1,300.00
   D. None of the above

10. Which of the following ownership interests applies to parties who own real property as tenants in common?
    A. The ownership interests must be equal.
    B. The ownership interests may be conveyed separately.
    C. The last surviving owner gets title to the property in severalty.
    D. The ownership interests may not be transferred by will or intestate distribution.

11. Which of the following terms identifies a property owner who has entered into an agency relationship with a licensee?
    A. Proxy
    B. Vendee
    C. Principal
    D. Fiduciary

12. A prospective buyer and an agent prepare an offer. The seller reviews the offer and accepts it with the provision that the closing date be changed by a month from the one proposed by the prospective buyer. Which of the following statements about this situation is CORRECT?
    A. There is a binding contract on the property.
    B. The prospective buyer is obligated to the terms but the seller is not.
    C. The seller has legally rejected the original offer and replaced it with a counteroffer.
    D. The closing date provision is not an essential part of a valid contract and violates the statute of frauds.

13. A residential property owner wants to buy a vacant lot next to the property to build a garage and small guesthouse. The lot has a recent appraisal of $10,000, but the property owner is prepared to pay more than that, if necessary, to be able to expand. Which of the following terms BEST identifies the amount this owner is willing to pay?
    A. Market price
    B. Market value
    C. Assessed value
    D. Actual cash value

14. When evaluating a property using the direct sales comparison (market data) approach, an amenity worth $5,000 in a comparable property is handled in which of the following ways?
    A. It is added to the subject property's estimated base value.
    B. It is subtracted from the comparable property's sales price.
    C. It is disregarded if it represents less than five percent of the comparable's value.
    D. It is averaged over the number of comparables used and added to the subject property.

15. Which of the following situations is MOST likely to be interpreted by an appraiser as a stigmatizing property condition?
    A. Substandard construction
    B. The presence of radon gas
    C. Undiscovered termite infestation
    D. A history of a major crime on the site

16. According to the common law of agency, which of the following statements about the fiduciary obligation of confidentiality is CORRECT when an agent represents a principal in a real estate transaction?
    A. It must be defined in writing to be legally valid.
    B. It outlasts the termination of the agency relationship.
    C. It is comparable to lawyer/client privilege and cannot be violated.
    D. It applies primarily to information about the principal's finances and motivation.

17. Barring any contractual agreement to the contrary, which of the following closing costs is MOST likely to be the responsibility of the seller?
    A. Recording fees
    B. Property insurance
    C. Agent compensation
    D. Lender's title insurance policy

18. A tenant who remains in a property against the wishes of the landlord after a lease period has expired is known as a
    A. joint tenant.
    B. tenant at will.
    C. periodic tenant.
    D. holdover tenant.

19. The term that BEST applies to the placement of client funds in a licensee's personal account is
    A. fraud.
    B. estoppel.
    C. commingling.
    D. embezzlement.

20. An appraiser determines that a subject thirty-year-old residence has a replacement cost of $185,000 and is on a parcel of land worth $47,000. The structure's accrued depreciation from physical deterioration and functional obsolescence is estimated at approximately 40%. Given this information, which of the following BEST represents the property's value?
    A. $139,200
    B. $158,000
    C. $213,200
    D. None of the above

21. Which of the following terms identifies the clause that allows a lender to call the entire remaining loan balance due in the event of buyer default?
    A. Novation
    B. Entitlement
    C. Acceleration
    D. Hypothecation

22. The owner of several convenience stores rents a small building for another store and installs built-in freezer units along the back wall. The term that BEST identifies these units is
    A. emblements.
    B. appurtenances.
    C. trade fixtures.
    D. personal property.

23. Which of the following types of listing agreements allows a seller to contract with multiple licensees and only compensate the one that produces the buyer?
    A. Net
    B. Open
    C. Exclusive
    D. Sole

24. A CORRECT statement about a promissory note used in the course of a real estate transaction is that it is
    A. an agency contract.
    B. a unilateral contract.
    C. a security instrument.
    D. a financing instrument.

25. Shortly after taking a property listing, the listing licensee is approached by a family member who asks the licensee to prepare an offer at a significantly reduced price. Under the common law of agency, the licensee MUST
    A. refuse to prepare or present this offer.
    B. attempt to get the relative to match the list price.
    C. discuss the potential conflict with an attorney prior to proceeding.
    D. disclose the family relationship of the potential buyer to the seller.

26. Which of the following changes in the immediate area of a home in a residential neighborhood with an aging population would be MOST likely to be characterized as depreciation due to external (economic) obsolescence?
    A. The closing of an elementary school
    B. The building of a new shopping mall
    C. The relocation of a medical center to another town
    D. The levying of a special assessment to replace aging sidewalks

27. According to the statute of frauds, in order for real estate sales contracts to be enforceable in court they MUST be
    A. recorded.
    B. witnessed.
    C. in writing.
    D. between competent parties.

28. A person who owns a house in severalty dies intestate. This person's spouse has also passed away, and one of their three children ran away from home and has not been heard from in over twenty years. Which of the following statements about the transfer of this property is CORRECT?
    A. The property will escheat to the state since the owner died intestate.
    B. The missing child represents a cloud on the title for future transfers.
    C. The two known children will receive a life estate interest in the property.
    D. The three children will be named as joint tenants with right of survivorship.

29. A homeowners insurance policy dated March 1 was issued for one year at a premium of $576. What is the prorated value of the unused portion as of November 15? (Use a 360-day year and 30-day months)
    A. $ 24
    B. $ 72
    C. $168
    D. None of the above

30. A licensee acting as a buyer's broker is preparing an offer for a buyer, who asks the licensee if there are any benefits to arranging seller-financing instead of going to a conventional lender. Which of the following statements represents the licensee's BEST response to this question?
    A. "Seller-financing may be better for the seller than for you."
    B. "I would have to look more closely at the other variables before I can give you an accurate answer."
    C. "The consequences of different kinds of financing do not vary enough to worry about it."
    D. "Make your best offer and include a contingency allowing you to review your options with an accountant or attorney."

31. Which of the following terms identifies the ownership of real property that is complete and has no restrictions on its use or transfer?
    A. Fee simple
    B. Abstract of title
    C. Severalty ownership
    D. Prior appropriation doctrine

32. As used in property management, the term "constructive eviction" is BEST understood to mean that a
    A. landlord is building a case against a tenant for eviction.
    B. court has made public its decision to support an eviction request.
    C. property has been sold and the tenant has been paid to vacate the premises.
    D. tenant has left a property after a landlord has allowed it to become uninhabitable.

33. When a building's value is calculated based on making an exact copy, this is known as the
    A. unit-in-place method.
    B. replacement cost method.
    C. reproduction cost method.
    D. capitalization rate method.

34. A property's appraised value is established in which of the following stages of the appraisal process?
    A. Reconciliation of data
    B. Definition of the problem
    C. Determination of highest and best use
    D. Applying the three approaches to value

35. What type of a contract is a real estate option contract?
    A. Void
    B. Implied
    C. Bilateral
    D. Unilateral

36. A homeowner hires a plumber to install a new bathroom and then refuses to pay. The plumber is entitled to take which of the following actions?
    A. Remove the plumbing
    B. Levy a special assessment
    C. Place a mechanic's lien on the property
    D. Petition the courts for a partition sale and recover the amount due from the proceeds

37. A percentage lease calls for a maximum monthly rental of $500 and 4% of the gross yearly sales over $60,000. Which of the following amounts represents the annual rent the tenant would pay in a year when the business had gross sales of $110,000?
    A. $2,200
    B. $4,400
    C. $6,000
    D. None of the above

38. A listing licensee discovers the listed property has a history of faulty plumbing that has never been adequately corrected. The licensee's responsibility regarding this information is that the licensee MUST
    A. include a reference to the plumbing in all advertising.
    B. disclose it only if asked directly by a prospective buyer.
    C. discuss it with the seller and disclose it to prospective buyers.
    D. treat it as confidential and disclose it only with the permission of the seller.

39. Which of the following government powers provides for the transfer of ownership of real property from an owner to the government in the event the property owner dies without a will or known heirs?
    A. Escheat
    B. Taxation
    C. Police power
    D. Eminent domain/compulsory purchase

40. A CORRECT statement about a title insurance premium paid at closing is that the premium represents
    A. the first of a series of annual payments.
    B. a one-time payment for the coverage purchased.
    C. a partial payment with the remainder due when the deed is recorded.
    D. a required charge to the seller if the property is being seller-financed.

41. Regarding lease agreements, which of the following statements represents a requirement of the statute of frauds as applied in Bermuda?
    A. All leases must include an adequate legal description of the property.
    B. Leases for more than three years must be in writing to be enforceable in court.
    C. The lessee must be renting the property for a legal purpose in order for the lease to be valid.
    D. An owner must rent substantially equivalent properties for similar rates to all tenants regardless of ethnic origin, sex, or age.

42. A buyer who receives a fee simple interest in an apartment unit and an undivided interest in the common areas held as tenants in common with the other unit owners has purchased a
    A. co-op.
    B. timeshare.
    C. townhouse.
    D. condominium.

43. Which of the following general property conditions is MOST likely to be categorized as material?
    A. A small attic
    B. A cracked foundation
    C. An exterior in need of paint
    D. An outdated set of kitchen appliances

44. A new property owner is clearing brush along an unmarked, overgrown property line and after clearing a few feet into a neighboring property begins to erect a fence along what the new owner believes to be the property line. This fence is an example of
    A. a lien.
    B. a licence.
    C. an encumbrance.
    D. an encroachment.

45. A deed is used during a settlement for which of the following purposes?
    A. Itemize all existing liens
    B. Verify the final sales price
    C. Warranty the chain of title
    D. Transfer property ownership

46. A key term that distinguishes personal property from real property is
    A. expense.
    B. location.
    C. mobility.
    D. ownership.

47. An investor asks a licensee to list a rental duplex at 10% more than it cost, including recent renovation expenses of $12,500. If the investor bought it two years ago for $146,300, what would the list price be?
    A. $147,180
    B. $158,800
    C. $160,930
    D. None of the above

48. The type of tenancy that allows either the tenant or the landlord to terminate it at any time without notice or penalty is a tenancy
    A. at will.
    B. in common.
    C. at sufferance.
    D. from period-to-period.

49. The term "usury" refers to which of the following practices?
    A. Using loan payment funds for a purpose that is either unethical or illegal
    B. Inflating standard loan discount, origination, or document preparation charges
    C. Recovering a share of losses from bad loans by increasing origination fees for new borrowers
    D. Charging an interest rate that is excessively, perhaps even illegally, higher than the market average

50. A property owner built a house on a 7,500 square foot lot several years prior to the enactment of new zoning that requires at least 20,000 square feet for residential properties in that area. A CORRECT statement about this situation is that the
    A. owner must purchase additional property to be in compliance.
    B. property represents a nonconforming use and nothing must be done.
    C. municipality must grant a variance to this property and others like it.
    D. title will have a cloud on it that must be removed prior to any future sale.

51. In the event one party to a real estate sales contract wants to back out, the other party may force the reluctant party to honor the terms of the contract through a legal process known as
    A. hypothecation.
    B. suit to quiet title.
    C. liquidated damages.
    D. specific performance.

52. The terms alluvial, littoral, and riparian refer to which of the following property rights?
    A. Air
    B. Water
    C. Mineral
    D. Improvements

53. According to basic contract law, unless there is a specific clause to the contrary, one effect of the sale of a leased property is that the lease is
    A. voided.
    B. no longer enforceable.
    C. binding on the new owner.
    D. subject to immediate renegotiation.

54. Which of the following types of deeds provides the GREATEST protection against title defects for the grantee?
    A. Quitclaim
    B. Special warranty
    C. General warranty
    D. Bargain and sale

55. A CORRECT statement about a leasehold estate interest in real property is that it
    A. must be recorded to be valid.
    B. transfers use but not ownership.
    C. creates a reversionary interest for the holder.
    D. allows the grantee to encumber the property.

56. Which of the following statements BEST defines the meaning of depreciation as it is used in appraisal?
    A. A loss of value resulting from any cause
    B. A decline in value due to economic factors
    C. The tendency of a property to lose value from overuse
    D. The deterioration of a property's structural integrity over time

57. The BEST statement about the relationship between a property mortgage and a promissory note is that the mortgage
    A. provides evidence of who made the loan to the property owner while the note identifies the face value of the loan.
    B. provides the details of the installment payments required for the loan while the note creates the legal liability for the repayment.
    C. creates a property lien as security for the note, which gives the details of both the amount of the debt and the terms of repayment.
    D. creates a public record of a property's indebtedness based on the note, which identifies the property location and credit history of the property owner.

58. A residential tenant has given a friend the right to take over the unit for the rest of the tenancy period. Which of the following terms BEST identifies what the original tenant has given the friend?
    A. Sublet
    B. Licence
    C. Assignment
    D. Tenancy at will

59. Assume that an entire calendar year's property taxes on land to be sold are due on December 31 and will be $1,500. If the closing on the sale will occur on September 15 and the seller pays for the day of closing, which of the following entries for prorated taxes is CORRECT? (Use a 360-day year and 30-day months.)
    A. Credit buyer $437.50
    B. Debit buyer $1,062.50
    C. Credit seller $437.50
    D. Debit seller $1,062.50

60. The involuntary alienation of real property is MOST likely to be seen when property title transfers by
    A. devise.
    B. reversion.
    C. remuneration.
    D. special warranty deed.

61. Which of the following financial arrangements represents an example of a real estate package loan?
    A. A line of credit is approved for home repairs
    B. A group of building lots are financed with a single loan
    C. A property loan includes an above-ground swimming pool as collateral
    D. A construction project is financed in installments as construction progresses

62. A property owner asks a licensee to list a property and says, "I need $40,000 from this sale; your compensation will be anything you can get over that amount." This is an example of which of the following types of listings?
    A. Net
    B. Open
    C. Exclusive
    D. Sole

63. The term "ad valorem" refers to which of the following areas of real estate?
    A. Property taxation
    B. Advertising requirements
    C. Commercial real estate
    D. Secondary mortgage markets

64. A lender is MOST likely to require a borrower to pay for private mortgage insurance in which of the following situations?
    A. The buyer has a history of bankruptcies.
    B. The property is within five feet of a primary road.
    C. The lender foreclosed on the property's past owner.
    D. The loan amount is for more than 80% of the property's value.

65. The type of tenancy that is created when a tenant leases a summer cabin for July, August, and September is known as a tenancy
    A. at will.
    B. for years.
    C. at sufferance.
    D. from period-to-period.

66. Which of the following types of deeds provides the LEAST protection against title defects for the grantee?
    A. Quitclaim
    B. Special warranty
    C. General warranty
    D. Bargain and sale

67. Under the terms of a typical gross lease, the tenant pays a fixed rent PLUS
    A. property taxes and utilities.
    B. property taxes and insurance.
    C. all increases in property taxes and assessments.
    D. nothing; the owner pays all other property-related expenses.

68. An investor's original investment of $252,000 produces a $975 weekly gross income from a property with monthly expenses of $2,535. The annualized return on this property is:
    A. 6%
    B. 8%
    C. 12%
    D. None of the above

69. A CORRECT statement about discount points charged by a lender is that the points
    A. increase the lender's overall yield on a loan.
    B. are prohibited for government-backed loans.
    C. are used by the lender to purchase mortgage insurance.
    D. will be returned to the borrower once the loan balance is paid off.

70. An appraisal would refer to a residence with four bedrooms and one bathroom as suffering from
    A. accrued depreciation.
    B. physical deterioration.
    C. functional obsolescence.
    D. external (economic) obsolescence.

71. A property owner lists a residence and specifically avoids telling the listing licensee about a leaking roof. The licensee notices water stains in a closet ceiling, but considers them old and never discusses them with either the owner or the buyer. The property is sold without disclosing this condition and the buyer sues for damages based on material misrepresentation. Do the seller and/or the licensee have any liability? Why or why not?
    A. Neither one is liable because the buyer has the obligation to have the property inspected.
    B. The seller is the only liable party because the licensee was never told about the problem.
    C. The seller and the licensee are both liable because the licensee is responsible for the actions of a principal.
    D. The seller and the licensee are both liable because it is reasonable that the licensee should have discovered this condition.

72. A property appraised at $264,000 includes land that is valued at $112,545. If the property is rectangular with boundaries of 265 feet by 185 feet, how much would a neighbor who wants to purchase a rectangular section measuring 265 feet by 50 feet expect to pay? (Round to the nearest $100.)
    A. $22,500
    B. $30,400
    C. $40,900
    D. None of the above

73. Which of the following situations BEST characterizes a property suffering from external (economic) obsolescence?
    A. A car dealership is located downwind of a new hog farm
    B. A house loses value due to leaking gutters and old wiring
    C. A school building is discovered to have asbestos problems
    D. A shopping center has an anchor tenant that goes bankrupt

74. In order to be valid, a contract for the sale of real estate MUST include which of the following elements?
    A. Offer and acceptance
    B. Financing information
    C. A definite termination date
    D. A "time is of the essence" clause

75. In the course of a real estate transaction, a bill of sale would be the BEST document for transferring the ownership of which of the following items?
    A. A fence
    B. A riding lawn mower
    C. Newly installed carpets
    D. Outbuildings on a large lot

76. During an open house, a listing licensee receives three offers, one of which is substantially less advantageous to the seller than the other two. According to the common law of agency, the licensee MUST present
   A. all offers.
   B. the offers the seller asks to see.
   C. each offer until the seller accepts one.
   D. only the two that are clearly best for the principal.

77. A buyer arranges for a $90,000 mortgage loan with an annual interest rate of 8% and a fixed monthly payment of $745. If the first loan payment is due 30 days after the loan origination date, how much of that payment will represent principal? (Use a 360-day year and 30-day months.)
   A. $125
   B. $145
   C. $600
   D. None of the above

78. A property manager's PRIMARY function for a property owner is to
   A. increase property revenues.
   B. decrease unit vacancy rates.
   C. achieve the owner's objectives.
   D. show space, prepare leases, and collect rents.

79. According to the common law of agency, a licensee has which of the following obligations to an individual that prefers to remain a customer rather than become a client?
   A. Confidentiality
   B. Courtesy and patience
   C. Honesty and fair dealing
   D. Only those agreed to in writing

80. Which of the following appraisal methods would be the MOST appropriate one to use in the valuation of a twenty-year-old post office?
   A. Cost
   B. Income
   C. Capitalization
   D. Direct sales comparison (market data)

81. A licensee takes an "as-is" listing on a residential property downhill from an abandoned industrial site. The licensee finds a buyer for the property who discovers after closing that residual industrial waste has been leaching into a small pond on the property for several years. In this situation, which of the following parties is MOST likely to have liability for the expense of correcting this problem?
    A. The new owner only
    B. The industrial property's owner only
    C. The former residence owner and the licensee only
    D. The industrial property owner, the former and current residence owners, and the licensee

82. Which of the following documents legally transfers the ownership of real property?
    A. A deed
    B. A bill of sale
    C. A lis pendens
    D. A certificate of estoppel

83. In Bermuda, the transfer of ownership through the process of compulsory purchase is an example of
    A. adverse possession.
    B. voluntary alienation.
    C. involuntary alienation.
    D. reclamation of abandoned property.

84. In performing a direct sales comparison (market data) analysis, an appraiser would be MOST interested in data on
    A. comparable properties.
    B. current cost of building materials.
    C. demographic changes in the community.
    D. local economic forces and population trends.

85. Which of the following statements BEST defines what is meant by the term "material defect"?
    A. Any condition that may change a principal's mind about buying or selling
    B. Any property defect that would cost more than 10% of the sales price to correct
    C. All conditions that add to a property's overall structural deterioration or depreciation in value
    D. All factors that the seller would prefer prospective buyers not to know about the seller's motivation

86. When acting in a fiduciary capacity for a seller in a real estate transaction, a licensee MUST
    A. be loyal to the seller's interests.
    B. obey all instructions of the seller.
    C. represent no other party in the transaction.
    D. disclose only those facts the seller wants known.

87. Which of the following interests in real property does a prospective buyer receive once an offer to purchase becomes a binding contract?
   A. Possession
   B. Ownership
   C. Equitable title
   D. Right to encumber

88. Which of the following elements MUST be included in a real estate contract in order for it to be legally valid?
   A. Consideration
   B. Proposed use of the property
   C. The covenant of quiet enjoyment
   D. Frequency and duration of any payments

89. Which of the following statements BEST defines real property?
   A. Land and the air space above it
   B. Land and its improvements and all included ownership rights
   C. Property that has been surveyed and identified by a full legal description
   D. All of the rights to land and improvements as identified in a property deed

90. Which of the following methods of transfer is MOST likely to represent the voluntary alienation of real property?
   A. Escheat
   B. Reversion
   C. Inheritance
   D. Foreclosure

91. A property lien is a type of
   A. easement.
   B. ownership.
   C. assessment.
   D. encumbrance.

92. Which of the following government powers provides for the acquisition of private land for public use, such as forcing an owner to sell some land for a road-widening project?
   A. Escheat
   B. Taxation
   C. Police power
   D. Compulsory purchase

93. A property deed indicates that the easternmost boundary includes a twelve-foot right of way allowing owners farther from the main road the right to cross the property. The property across which the others are allowed to pass is known as a
    A. subdivided parcel.
    B. landlocked parcel.
    C. servient tenement.
    D. dominant tenement.

94. Property managers often have been granted a wide range of job-related authority to act on behalf of their principal. This is known as which of the following types of agency?
    A. Special
    B. General
    C. Universal
    D. Subagency

95. Barring any contractual agreement to the contrary, which of the following closing costs is MOST likely to be the responsibility of the buyer?
    A. Discount points
    B. Mechanic's liens
    C. Mortgage balance payoff
    D. Real estate brokerage fees

96. A property sold for $227,500 with a 5% commission paid by the seller for brokerage services. The listing company retained 60% of the commission and the buyer's agent received 55% of the compensation paid to the buyer's company. In this situation, the buyer's company netted how much on this sale?
    A. $1,993.25
    B. $2,047.50
    C. $2,502.50
    D. None of the above

97. Which of the following loan-related terms identifies a final loan payment that is generally much larger than any of the ones before?
    A. Term
    B. Swing
    C. Balloon
    D. Nonrecourse

98. Which of the following types of contract clauses is MOST likely to be included in a lease to allow a landlord to raise the rent periodically?
    A. Extension
    B. Escalation
    C. Assignment
    D. Acceleration

99. Which of the following types of leases provides for the tenant to pay a base rent and some of the property expenses, such as utilities, maintenance, and taxes?
    A. Net
    B. Index
    C. Gross
    D. Graduated

100. Which of the following types of insurance provides a new property owner with the BEST protection against the risk of loss due to claims brought by previously undiscovered prior owners?
    A. Title
    B. Property
    C. Casualty
    D. Homeowners

This is the end of the Sample Questions.

The answers for the Sample Exam Questions are on the following page.

Please check your work closely before turning to the next page and scoring your answers.

Appendix C: Answer Key and Content Code Areas for Sample Questions

Sample Questions: Answer Key and Content Code Areas
Math questions are indicated with an *

#	Key	Sec	#	Key	Sec	#	Key	Sec	#	Key	Sec
1.	B	I(A)	26.	C	I(C)	51.	D	I(D)	76.	A	II(C)
2.	C	I(C)	27.	C	I(D)	52.	B	I(A)	77.	B	I(E)*
3.	D	I(F)	28.	B	I(F)	53.	C	I(D)	78.	C	I(H)
4.	A	I(G)	29.	C	I(G)*	54.	C	I(F)	79.	C	II(C)
5.	B	II(A)	30.	D	II(C)	55.	B	I(D)	80.	A	I(C)
6.	B	I(E)	31.	A	I(A)	56.	A	I(C)	81.	D	II(C)
7.	C	II(D)	32.	D	I(H)	57.	C	I(F)	82.	A	I(F)
8.	B	I(G)	33.	C	I(C)	58.	A	I(D)	83.	C	I(B)
9.	C	I(H)*	34.	A	I(C)	59.	D	I(G)*	84.	A	I(C)
10.	B	I(A)	35.	D	I(D)	60.	B	I(A)	85.	A	II(C)
11.	C	II(A)	36.	C	I(B)	61.	C	I(E)	86.	A	II(B)
12.	C	I(D)	37.	D	I(H)*	62.	A	I(D)	87.	C	I(D)
13.	A	I(C)	38.	C	II(C)	63.	A	I(B)	88.	A	I(D)
14.	B	I(C)	39.	A	I(B)	64.	D	I(E)	89.	B	I(A)
15.	D	I(C)	40.	B	I(F)	65.	B	I(D)	90.	C	I(B)
16.	B	II(B)	41.	B	I(D)	66.	A	I(F)	91.	D	I(B)
17.	C	I(G)	42.	D	I(A)	67.	D	I(D)	92.	D	I(B)
18.	D	I(D)	43.	B	II(C)	68.	B	I(H)*	93.	C	I(A)
19.	C	I(G)	44.	D	I(A)	69.	A	I(E)	94.	B	II(A)
20	B	I(C)*	45.	D	I(F)	70.	C	I(C)	95.	A	I(G)
21.	C	I(E)	46.	C	I(A)	71.	D	II(C)	96.	B	I(G)*
22.	C	I(A)	47.	D	I(H)*	72.	B	I(C)*	97.	C	I(E)
23.	B	I(D)	48.	A	I(D)	73.	A	I(C)	98.	B	I(D)
24.	D	I(F)	49.	D	I(E)	74.	A	I(D)	99.	A	I(D)
25.	D	II(C)	50.	B	I(B)	75.	B	I(G)	100.	A	I(F)

Remember – when reviewing your answers, pay special attention to the distractors. Many of them will be "real" answers on the real exam!

Notes

About the Author

John R. Morgan entered the field of large-volume test development at the Educational Testing Service (ETS) in Princeton, New Jersey where he spent several years writing, editing, and assembling material for the verbal portion of the Scholastic Aptitude Test (SAT), Advanced Placement Literature examinations, and other national examination programs.

A professional educator and writer since receiving his Master of Arts in Teaching English from Brown University in 1981, Morgan took his first real estate course in 1978 while studying literature at the University of Connecticut. He held his first real estate license in Rhode Island during graduate school, his second in Arizona, where he sold property in Tucson, and now holds his third in his native Connecticut, where he currently lives with his wife and two young sons on Long Island Sound's eastern shores.

After leaving ETS and selling real estate in Tucson, Morgan moved to Philadelphia to work for Assessment Systems, Incorporated (ASI), where he spent over three and one-half years in its Real Estate Test Development program.

During this time, Morgan was in charge of developing, maintaining, and enhancing all question pools and license exams for ASI's then 20+ real estate client jurisdictions by conducting over two dozen state-specific test development meetings and consultations in capitals from Massachusetts and Rhode Island to Washington, Alaska, and Hawaii.

His career at ASI culminated in drafting an encompassing general outline based on a national job analysis, then reviewing it and all of ASI's sales-level test questions with a national committee of Subject Matter Experts. This outline and question-pool, with some recent modifications, is still in use by ASI's successor company, Pearson VUE.

Morgan left ASI in early 1998 to found Morgan Testing Services and pursue consulting, writing, and other service opportunities. He has reviewed and/or revised thousands of test questions in many of Dearborn Publishing Company's real estate prelicensing publications, written nine books, and prepared secure end-of-course sales, broker, and property manager examinations for Realtors Associations and other private prelicensing schools.

Further, he has prepared and facilitated curriculum development workshops for the state of South Carolina, an instructor workshop on question-writing for the North Carolina Real Estate Commission, an exam-bank development presentation for a Connecticut Instructors Seminar, and several question-writing seminars for annual meetings of the Real Estate Educators' Association (REEA).

As a consultant, he has also provided test development services and licensing exams for the states of Arizona, Pennsylvania, and South Carolina as well as the government of Bermuda, and has served on the Connecticut Real Estate Commission's Educational Advisory Committee. In addition, Morgan was nominated and selected for inclusion since 2008 in the annual publication of "Who's Who in America" along with "Who's Who in the World" since 2009.